Hamlyn Hobby Horses
COLLECTING

Written by Jennifer Curry
Illustrated by Sarah Hale
Photographs by Philip James

HAMLYN
London · New York · Sydney · Toronto

Also in the
Hamlyn Hobby Horse series
Printing

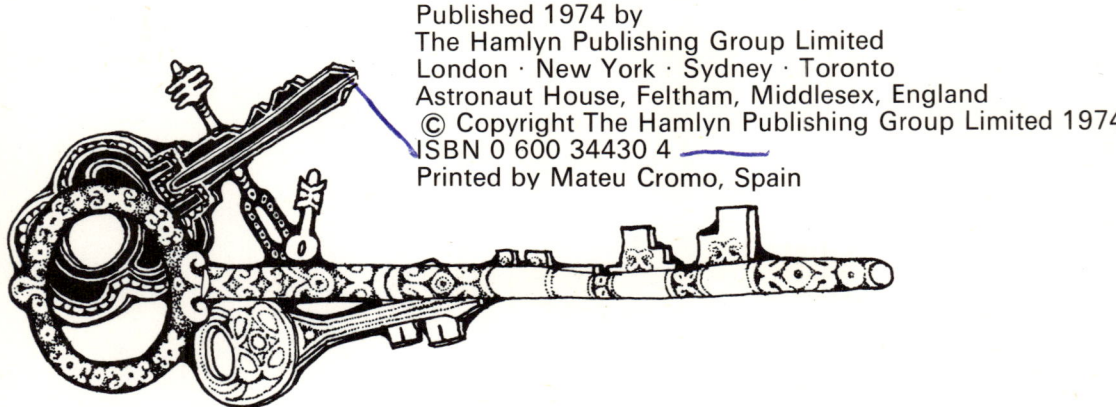

Published 1974 by
The Hamlyn Publishing Group Limited
London · New York · Sydney · Toronto
Astronaut House, Feltham, Middlesex, England
© Copyright The Hamlyn Publishing Group Limited 1974
ISBN 0 600 34430 4
Printed by Mateu Cromo, Spain

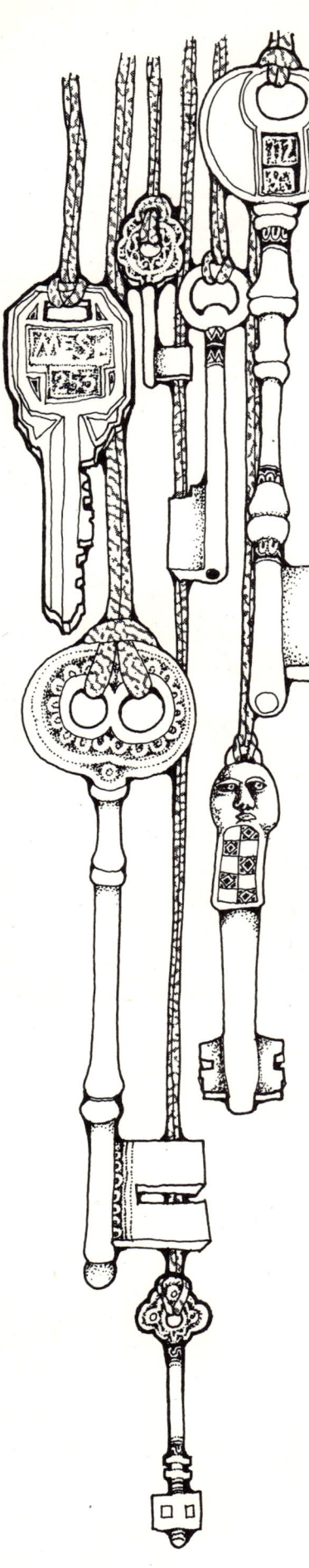

CONTENTS

Leaves

Have you ever thought about collecting *leaves*?

It is a very good idea, because they are easy to find, and cost you nothing. Any park, wood or garden will give a fine start to your collection.

They can be preserved and displayed in many different ways, they can be made up into a variety of attractive things, and they will help you to discover all sorts of interesting facts about the natural world around you.

When you begin to collect leaves you could make a picture record of your collection in a loose-leaf scrap-book.

ASPEN

EVERGREEN OAK.

Here is one way of doing it. From each different type of tree, pick the most perfect leaf you can find. Lay each leaf, its veins facing upwards, on newspaper, and cover it with a sheet of thin white paper. Now rub a soft pencil or crayon over the top of the leaf, always moving it in the same direction, until you have made a *scribble print*. Cut this out carefully, stick it in your scrap-book, and write beside it: the *name* of the tree, the *place* where you found it growing and the *date* you collected it. If you can, add a drawing of the tree, its flower and its fruit.

Another way is to put the leaves themselves into your scrap-book, but first you must *press* them. Lay them between sheets of blotting-paper underneath a pile of books, or the carpet, and leave them for a week or so. Or you can press the blotting-paper with a warm iron until the leaves are stiff and dry. Afterwards you will be able to fasten them into your scrap-book with a dab of glue, or a strip of clear sticky tape. Tissue paper between the pages will help protect them.

If your leaf comes from a tree which loses its leaves every year it is a good idea to collect one specimen when it is fresh and green, and another a few months later, just before it is ready to fall, to record how the colours have changed. Can you find out *why* the colours have changed?

Pressed leaves will last a long time if they are not handled too much, so you can use them in many ways.

You can mount them on pieces of folded card to make your own greeting cards and notelets, covering them with thin transparent plastic to protect them. Add ribbon and a glitter edging if you want to give them an extra decorative finish for a special occasion.

Or arrange your leaves in an attractive spray on a larger piece of card, add a ribbon loop at the top, and a calendar tab at the bottom, and your leaves will give pleasure a whole year through.

You might like to design a collage, which will last even longer. Choose the most attractive and interesting leaf-sprays you have, taking care to include leaves of different colours, shapes and sizes. Try to find an old picture frame — there might be one lying about the house, or you could buy one at a junk shop or jumble sale — and cut a piece of stiff card to fit inside it exactly. Arrange the sprays in a pattern on the card, and stick them into position with tiny blobs of transparent glue. Now fit the card inside the frame, making sure that it is firmly fastened into place at the back with sticky tape.

If you have a chest or dressing-table with a sheet of glass on the top you can arrange leaves under the glass to make it look very pretty. Or you can make a finger-plate. Stick a few leaves on to a piece of card, fasten this to the edge of the door just by the handle, and cover it with one of the special perspex finger panels that you can buy quite cheaply in a hardware store.

You could arrange leaves in the same way on a piece of card cut and shaped to fit into the bottom of an old tea-tray. Stick it down firmly, cover it with a sheet of self-adhesive transparent vinyl — and you will have given the tray an unusual new look.

This same clear vinyl can be used to make bookmarks. Cut a piece of card into an oval shape about 9 in (20 cm) long and 1½ in (4 cm) wide. Arrange some pretty leaves on it and press down the vinyl over the top, trimming the edges to make it fit the card exactly. Fasten a long piece of ribbon to the back, cutting a V-notch in the streamer ends so that they don't fray.

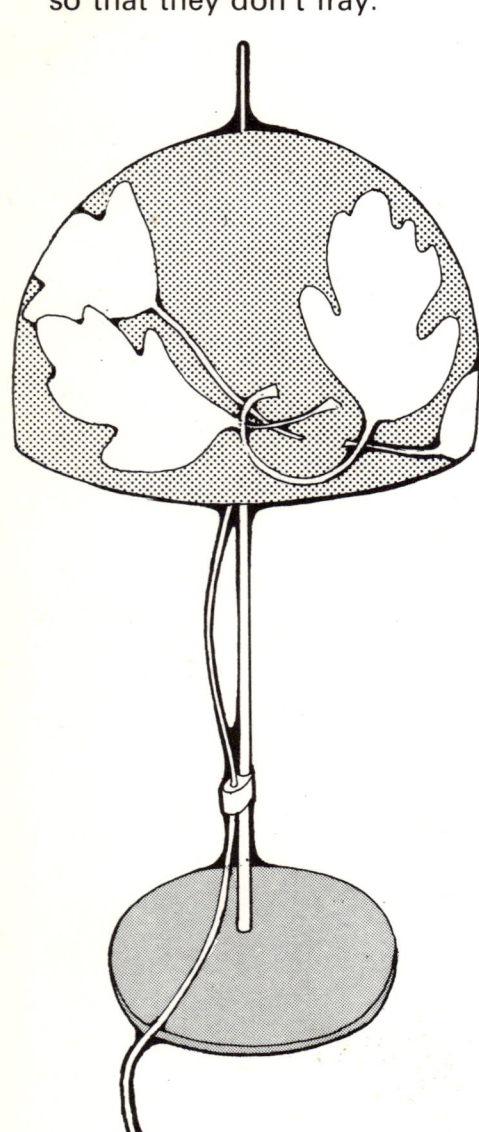

The shapes and colours of leaves look lovely when light shines through them — just look up at a leafy tree when the sun is glinting through its branches. It is possible to use artificial light to create the same effect. One way is to make a pattern of leaves on a plain lamp-shade, sticking them on carefully with a few small dabs of transparent glue. When the lamp is lit the leaves will glow with colour, and their various shapes will stand out very clearly.

You can do all these things with leaves you have *pressed*, but there are other ways of preserving them. If you want sprays of beech, maple and oak to look fresh and natural for a long time you should use the *glycerine* method. Collect the sprays quite late in the year, just before the leaves begin to fall. Hammer the ends of the twigs, then stand them in a mixture of one part of glycerine and two parts of warm water, which must be at least 4 in (10 cm) deep, leaving them to soak for two weeks. Then they will be ready to use in dried flower arrangements and decorations.

When leaves fall from the trees their soft parts rot away before their veins and they become 'skeletons'. Skeleton leaves are very strange, beautiful and delicate. It is not easy to find many that are in perfect condition, and even if you do, they often crumble away when you touch them. But you can skeletonise your fresh leaves by soaking them in a hot, but not quite boiling, solution, of about one teaspoonful of caustic soda to one pint of water, until the fleshy parts begin to come away. Go on pulling the flesh from the veins until the skeletons are quite bare, then rinse them very thoroughly under running water until every trace of caustic soda has gone, and pat dry between sheets of blotting paper. Be very careful with this solution, caustic soda can burn your hands.

Use your skeleton leaves to make an attractive display by mounting them on a wall-chart of thick coloured paper, or stick them into your scrap-book beside green or coloured leaves taken from the same tree.

11

If you like the idea of designing your own decorated paper, you can use leaves for several painting and printing techniques. You have already learnt how to make scribble prints with pencil and coloured crayons. Now try *paint-printing.* Choose a leaf that has veins which stand out clearly and stick it, upside down, on to a small piece of card. Using a brush or sponge, cover the leaf with a thick layer of poster paint, then press the painted surface firmly on to a sheet of dampened paper and build up an all-over pattern of leaf prints.

You can also use a leaf as a *stencil*. Hold it firmly against your paper, dip your brush in paint, and apply it to the edges of the leaf, working outwards from the centre. Move the leaf around the paper, changing its position and using different colours, until you have made an exciting picture.

By now you will have built up a collection of beautiful hand-decorated paper which you will be able to use in many different ways. It will wrap gifts, make covers and end-papers for your books and files, posters for your walls, and lining for your drawers and shelves.

It will also make a unique record of your hobby of collecting leaves.

Spatter work is another technique to try. Pin some leaves into position on a sheet of paper, and spray it with paint or ink so that the whole surface is covered with tiny dots. When the colour is dry take the leaves off, and cover the paper with an all-over spray of another colour. If you can't find an old household spray for this project, use a tooth-brush and comb instead. Just dip the brush into paint, hold it over the paper, and pull the bristles back with the comb. But don't forget to spread some newspaper over the table before you start, because this can be a messy business.

Wild Flowers and Grasses

If you read the section about leaves, you will see that many of the ideas there can work just as well with a collection of *wild flowers.*

Start by making a loose-leaf scrap-book of flowers that you have pressed by either the 'heavy-weight' or 'warm-iron' method.

Look for wild flowers whenever you go for a walk, but never pick more than two or three. You should always leave some growing so that they can seed themselves and flower again another year.

Collect the best specimens you can see, if possible with both buds and open flowers, and a few leaves to go with them. Wrap their stems in damp cotton wool, put them in a polythene bag or a jam jar until you get home, then press them as soon as possible.

You might prefer to make wall-charts of coloured card or thick paper. Each chart could be restricted to flowers of one particular habitat, using a different colour for each different group. Decorate the edges with pictures which represent the scenery of the place where the flowers were picked, add drawings of the birds, animals and insects that live there, and you will have made a very gay poster.

When you put a new flower in your scrap-book print beside it its name, the name and description of the place where you found it growing and the date you picked it.

It is a good idea to divide your scrap-book into several sections, keeping one for woodland flowers, another for hedgerow flowers, another for sea-side flowers, and so on. You will be surprised by the variety of homes, or *habitats*, that flowers find for themselves.

You will only want a few of the flowers you collect for your scrap-book or wall-charts, but there are many ways you can use the others. You can make them into the greetings cards, calendars, collages and finger-plates as described for leaves, and they, too, will look very beautiful laid on the plain surface of a dressing table or tray, under a piece of glass or clear vinyl.

Some could be used to make a set of coasters or table mats. Cut squares of cork or hardboard to the size you need, stick a piece of felt on one side, and thin coloured card on the other. Mount a pressed flower in the centre of the card, and gently smooth over the whole square a piece of sticky, transparent vinyl, cut to exactly the same size. Finish off by sticking a trimming of braid around the edges.

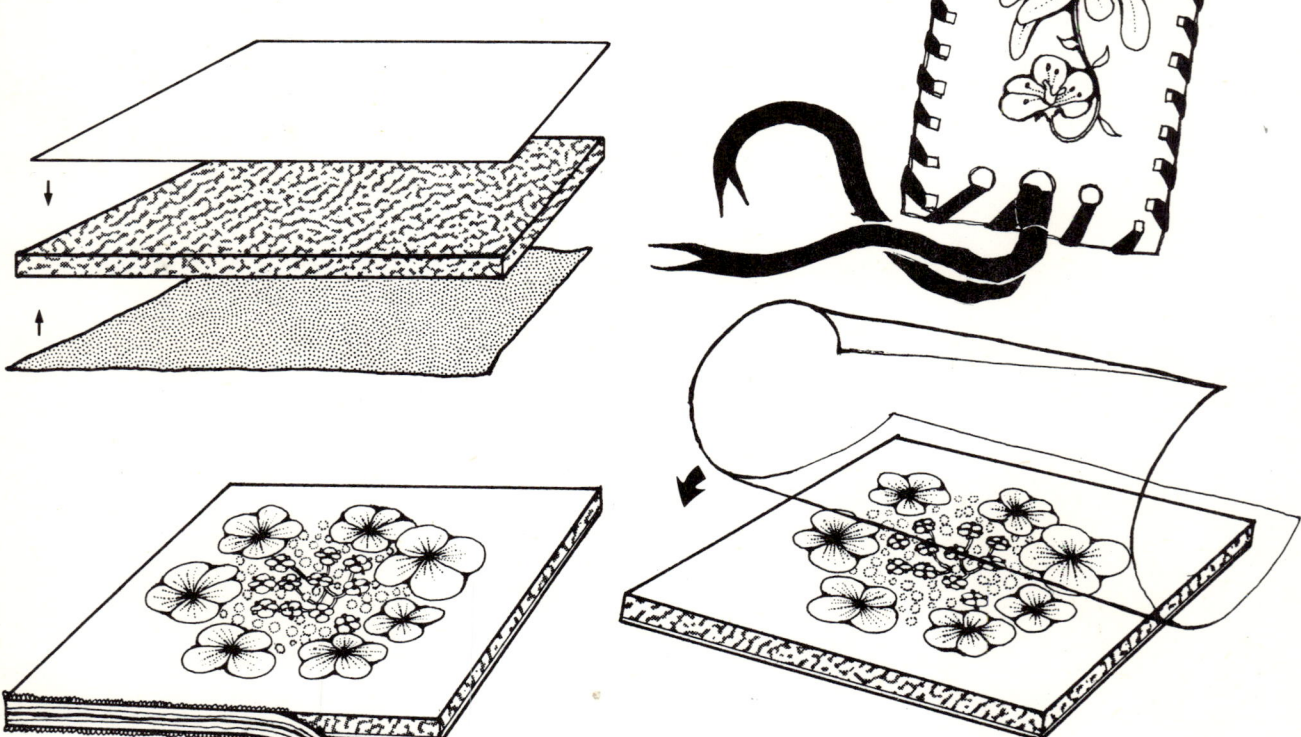

You can make bookmarks like those made with leaves, but use a slightly different method with flowers, so that their perfume can escape. Put a sweet-smelling pressed flower between two pieces of thick transparent plastic cut to the shape and size of your choice, fastening it into place with a spot of glue. Punch holes around the edges, lace the pieces together with narrow ribbon or cord, then knot the two ends together, leaving them to hang down at the bottom to form a tassel.

If you use your imagination you can make very unusual pictures with pressed flowers. You will need two sheets of card, both the same size, a pencil, paints and glue, pressed flowers and leaves, and a small piece of ribbon. First of all, draw an edging of half an inch (1 cm) round one piece of card, and keep your picture within this frame. Now paint on a background of blue sky and green lawns, and leave to dry. When you have done that, sort out the shapes of your petals and leaves, and glue them on to your painted background to build up a picture. For instance, some leaves can look like trees; large petals can be arranged to imitate a lady's skirt or parasol, or a cloud; tiny ones can look like puffs of smoke, or a cobbled path. Little flowers fixed in the foreground will give the impression of distance. Any extra details that you can't manage to capture with petal shapes can be drawn in at the end. Finally, measure a half-inch (1 cm) edging round your second piece of card and cut away the centre to leave a narrow frame. Stick this down firmly first fitting in a ribbon loop at the top.

We have already described how to *press* flowers. You can also try some of the other ways of preserving them, such as the *borax method.* The flowers should be almost fully-open, in perfect condition, and absolutely dry, and have had all their leaves removed. Cover the bottom of a box with borax, and place the flowers on it, heads downwards. Sprinkle more powder around them until they are completely covered. Put the box in the warmest, driest place possible for a week or so, and take the flowers out as soon as they are quite dry. You will be able to use the borax again and again, for more flowers.

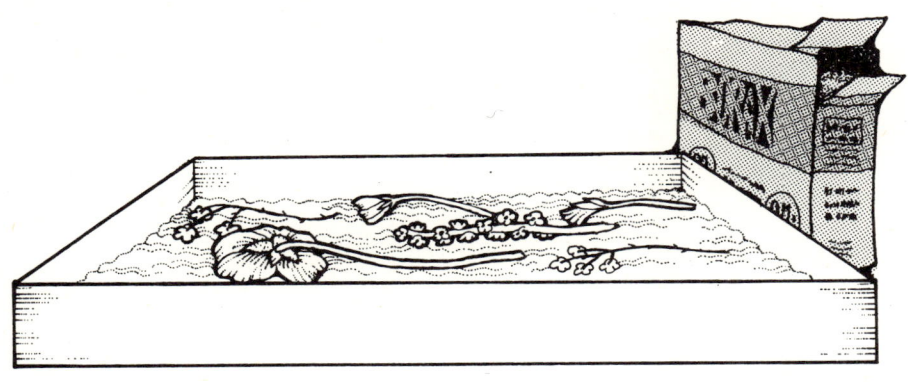

Many flowers, grasses and seed-heads will dry by the *natural method* if you hang them upside down in bunches in a dry, airy cupboard away from bright light. Look out especially for heathers, thistles, mullein, loose-strife, corn-flowers, large daisies, reeds, wheat, barley and oats, and the seedheads of bluebells, cowparsley, docks, poppies and teazles. Old Man's Beard should be preserved by the *glycerine method* used for leaves, described on page 11, and then sprayed with hair lacquer to protect it.

If you would like to dye some of your dried flowers just dip them in hot, but not boiling, household dye, leave for half an hour, rinse, and hang them up to dry.

To give them a special look for parties or Christmas, spray them with gold or silver paint, or dip them into white emulsion paint and sprinkle them with glitter powder before they are quite dry.

You will now have a supply of beautiful wild flowers and grasses that you can use in all sorts of ways. You could mount either whole sprays, or flower and seed-heads alone, on to a piece of thick card and frame it to make a lovely collage. You could arrange them on a piece of coloured hessian, looped over a bamboo cane, and fasten it up as a wall-hanging. Or you could design some lovely flower arrangements.

Oops-a-daisy

Get 4 styrofoam or oasis bricks from the flower department of a big store, stick them together to make a cube, then round off the top corners with a sharp knife. Stick pins through dried daisy-heads into the dome until the styrofoam is completely covered with a mass of flowers.

Harvest moon

Twist loops of fine wire around pieces of Old Man's Beard and ears of corn and barley. Stick them all over a big crescent-shaped piece of styrofoam as shown on the opposite page. Fasten a length of white ribbon through a wire loop pressed into the top, to hang it from the ceiling where it will twist and turn.

So far, we have been thinking about the look and perfume of wild flowers, but many of them are delicious to taste too, and can be used in cookery. Here are just two of my favourite flower recipes for you to try.

Elderflower fritters

You will need: 25 white elderflower clusters
                          icing sugar
                          salt
                          fat, for frying

for the batter   4 oz (100 g) flour
                          $\frac{1}{2}$ tspn salt
                          2 eggs
                          $\frac{1}{2}$ pint (250 ml) milk
                          1 tspn melted butter

Wash the flower clusters in a large bowl of cold, salted water. Remove the stems and leaves without breaking the clusters. Drain the flowers on kitchen paper.

Make batter by sieving flour into a bowl, making a well in the centre and breaking the eggs into it. Stir with a wooden spoon, adding milk a little at a time. Add salt and butter and beat until smooth and creamy. Dip each flower cluster into it and fry in deep hot fat until golden brown, taking great care not to splash the fat. Sprinkle with icing sugar and serve hot.

Candied violets

You will need: a large bunch of violets
                          2 egg whites
                          8 oz (225 g) granulated sugar

Wash the flowers, keeping them whole, but removing the stems and green parts. Pat them dry on kitchen paper. Beat the egg whites until they are foamy but not stiff, and dip the flowers in, coating them all over. Next dip the flowers in sugar, coating them thoroughly, before placing them on grease-proof paper.

Dry them out thoroughly in a warm place, and store them in an airtight jar. Use them as decorations for cakes or puddings, or eat them as sweets. This recipe works with red rose petals too.

Cones

Cones are the fruits of *conifers*, the name given to all the different sorts of trees that produce cones. Pine trees, firs, cedars, cypress, larch are all conifers – and each of these separate tree families has several members. For instance, there are Scots pines, Austrian pines and Corsican pines; Douglas firs and silver firs; cedars of Lebanon and Indian cedars . . . and so on.

Cones are fun to collect because they are easily found, in all sorts of different shapes and sizes, and their scales are easily cut and painted, so you can model with them, and use them in many decorative ways.

It would be a good idea to start your collection by keeping a record of those you find in a book. On each page draw a picture of a particular conifer, and add smaller drawings of the sort of cone it bears, and a leaf spray. At the bottom of the page write the name of the tree and the sort of place it grows. Try to find out what the wood of the tree is used for.

Divide your record book into sections, keeping each family group together, and whenever you find a cone, look through your book to see what sort of conifer it has come from and write down, on the same page, where and when you collected it.

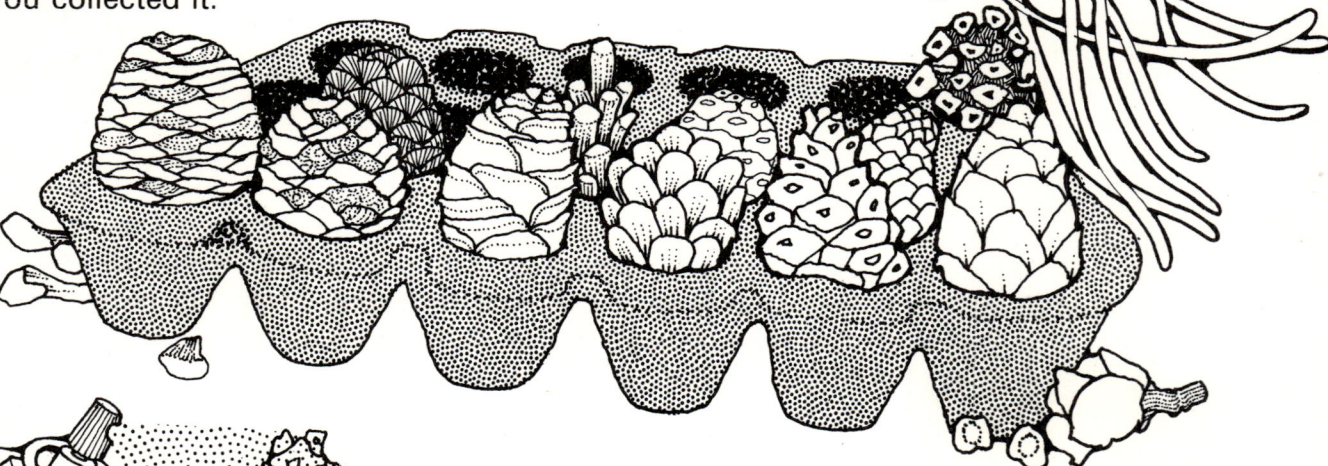

Cones are easy to find. You will see them either clinging to their parent tree, even after the wind has shaken out their seeds, or lying on the soil beneath. Only collect perfect cones. Throw away the ones that are damaged, or have been nibbled by animals. Brush your specimens clean, and leave them in a warm place to dry out before you start working with them because, as you will discover, their shapes change in the atmosphere. You can arrange your cones very neatly in a shallow drawer or box, if you line it with egg-boxes. Stick a label at the top of each separate hollow and print on it the name of the sort of cone that will be kept there.

Some cones can be added to displays of dried flowers if you fasten fine wire around them, between the scales, and twist the ends together to make a wire stalk.

For a table display you could make up an autumn collage. Arrange a group of natural objects in a pattern on a pretty, shallow dish or board, combining your cones with pebbles, shells, bare branches or pieces of bark, and trailing ivy, dried grasses and seedheads, stuck into a foil-covered potato to hold them in position.

It is very easy to brighten up your cones if you wish. For instance, you can dip them into white emulsion paint and sprinkle them with glitter powder before they are quite dry. Or you can paint them with vivid enamels, or spray them silver or gold. If you prefer the cones their original colour you can give them a shine, and keep them in good condition, by applying a coat of clear varnish.

Christmas garland

For a garland, bend a wire coat-hanger into a perfect circle, then twist around it lengths of ivy, held in place with clear sticky tape. Fasten on clusters of fir cones, wired and painted white, then tie a bow of red ribbon around the hook, letting the streamers float down over the wreath.

Golden tree

To make a tree you will need to fill a large plastic cream carton with plaster, push in a 10 in (25 cm) length of thin dowelling, and leave it to set hard. Then spread glue around the top of the dowelling, and press down on it a medium-sized ball of wool. Wire small, opened, fir cones, and push the wire stalks firmly into the wool, until the ball is completely covered. Now spray the tree and pot all over with gold paint, and tie a bow of coloured ribbon around the bottom of the 'trunk'.

At Christmas time, cones make attractive decorations. Some can be hung on the Christmas Tree. Others can be used for a Christmas log if you mix plaster-of-Paris and pour it over a log that is an interesting shape. Before it is set, stick into it a few cones, a coloured candle and two or three glass baubles, finishing off with sprigs of greenery.

Figure-modelling with cones is becoming a very popular hobby, and it is not difficult. If you use small cones or nuts as heads, and large cones as bodies, use pipe-cleaners for flexible arms, legs and tails, tiny buttons or beads for eyes, scraps of felt for ears and clothes, and wool for hair, you will soon see the possibility of building up a large collection of birds, animals, monsters, fairies, and human figures. Here are instructions for a few, just to start you off.

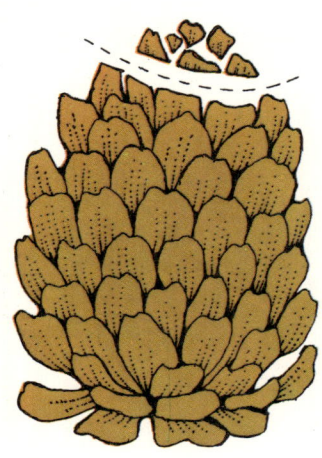

Owl

Hold a large, round, opened cone upwards and make a slight hollow in the top by cutting out the tips of the topmost scales. Add two yellow eyes and two pointed felt ears to a small round cone, and fasten this head into the hollow.

Penguin

Keep the larger of two pointed cones upright, with the little stem at the back as a tail, and fasten feet made of two scales to the bottom. Turn the smaller cone on its side, carve a hollow in the widest part of it, and fit this over the top of the larger cone, making it point the same way as the feet, then glue the two together. Add eyes, paint a broad white 'waistcoat' down the front, and colour the rest of the penguin black.

Witch

Put a small cone on top of a larger, narrow one which has had its base cut off to make it stand firm, and paint this head and body black. Glue on black wool hair, and green bead eyes, and make a pointed black hat from paper and stick it in place. Push a pipe-cleaner through the top of the bigger cone to form two arms, and curve the ends to form hands. Now make your witch a tiny broomstick, from a bit of twig and some dried grass, or straw. Let her fly on her broomstick, hanging from a black thread.

Ballet dancer

Turn a large opened cone upside down and twist a pipe-cleaner round the topmost scales to form a head. Cut out some scales from the middle, to shape a waist. Add pipe-cleaner arms and legs, twisted into a dancing position. Give your dancer a tissue-paper tu-tu, and hang her up by a thread.

Man

Chop the top off a large thin cone and join the top and bottom together by glueing them to a small stick 'neck'. Give the man pipe-cleaner arms and legs, and a tiny twiggy walking stick.

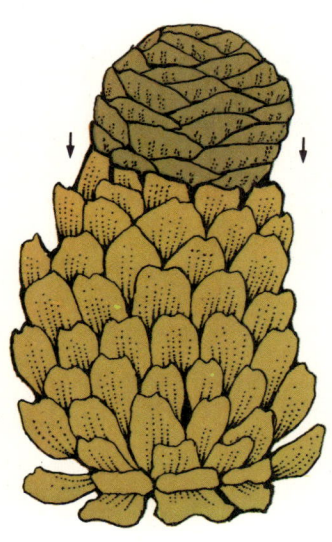

Dog

For the dog's body use a large pointed cone, turned on its side, the point forming its tail. Fasten a small pointed cone to the front, the pointed end being its nose. Glue on pointed scales, upright, for ears, and add brown button eyes. Push two pipe-cleaners through the cone from one side to the other, and twist them down to act as legs, turning the ends round slightly for big flat feet.

Another way of displaying cones is to fasten thread around them and hang them from the ceiling, or the underside of a shelf, or to make them up into a mobile.

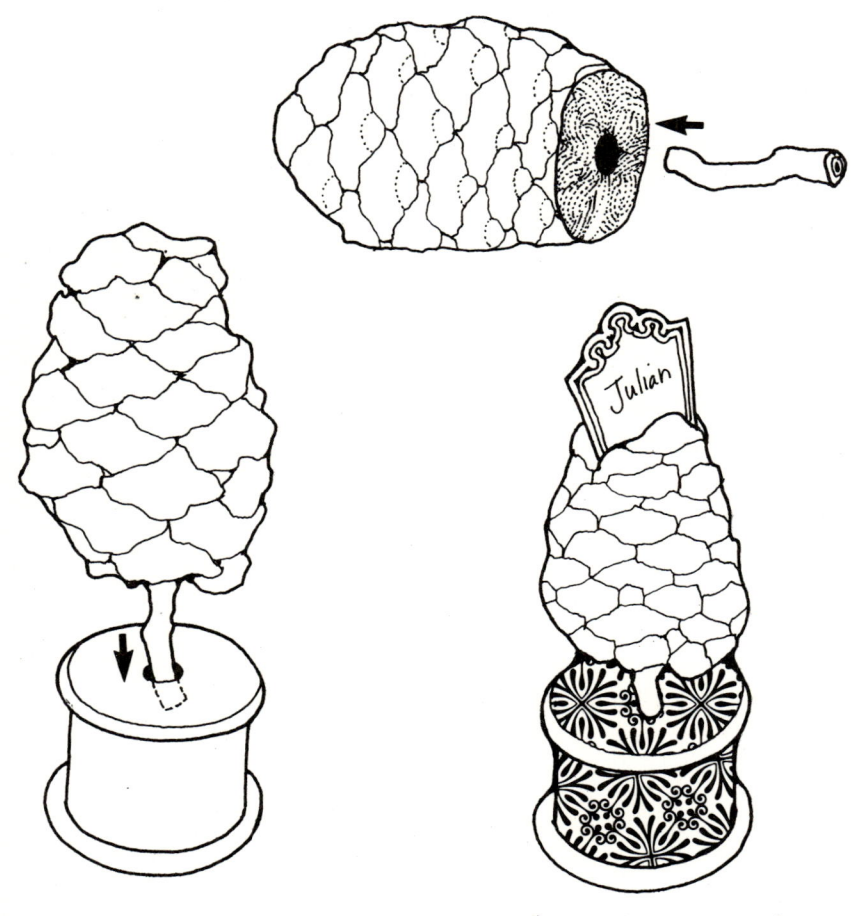

You can also make your cones into tiny trees for a miniature garden. If you have some, use green unripened cones picked from the branches while they are still closed up. If not, soak some opened cones in water for a few hours until they have closed, dry them thoroughly, then paint them with clear varnish so that they will not open out again. Cut off the bottom of each cone, make a hole in the base, and glue into it a little piece of twig. Stick the other end of the twig into a brightly painted cotton reel. If you make a narrow slit across the top of the cone you can put a piece of card into it and use it as a place-marker for a party.

Your tiniest cones can be used to decorate screw-top jars, tins or boxes that you have painted. Bigger ones can make an attractive decoration for a pair of plain book-ends, or an unusual edging for a picture or mirror.

Pebbles & Stones

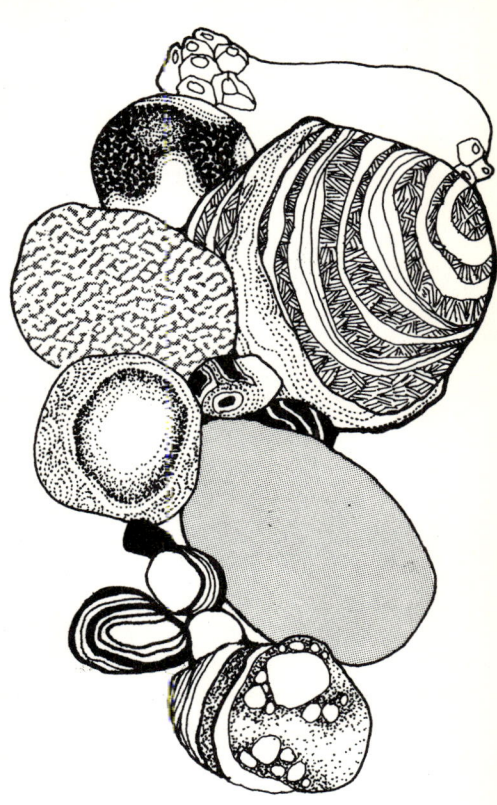

You must have walked by the sea sometimes, or along a river bank, and been delighted by the colours and shapes of the pebbles and stones you saw there.

Perhaps you brought some home, but didn't quite know what to do with them, and were disappointed to discover that, though their colours glowed beautifully when they were wet, they looked dull and rather uninteresting when they had dried.

There are several ways of showing off stones to their best advantage. The first is to 'polish' them with a special machine. Unfortunately, these are rather expensive, but there might be one at school you could use.

Another is to keep them in water. Scrub the pebbles clean, put them in a pretty glass jar with a lid and cover them with water. You can label each jar with the name of the place where the pebbles were collected, using different jars for different places. They will look so beautiful and unusual that you will be able to use them as ornaments.

Soon you will begin to recognise the different types of stone you are finding. For instance, you may have some granite in your collection, in different colours of pinks, greys and yellows. There could be flint, sandstone, limestone, even quartz, which is very lovely. Try to break some of them open so that you can find out what they look like inside. Then get a book from your library, or visit the local museum, and see if you can discover their names and characteristics. Pick out the best specimens you have and put them in egg boxes, labelling each separate hollow with the name of the stone, and the date and place it was found. See how many different ones you can collect.

You can use all the extra pebbles you gather to make some very attractive things, especially if you include the coloured glass you often find, worn quite smooth by the action of the sea. You would probably enjoy making a pebble-mosaic on a board with straight-edged lengths of wooden beading glued round it to make a frame. A small one will make a plant stand. A larger one can be hung on the wall.

If you are going to use the mosaic as a stand, stick a piece of felt on the bottom. If you are going to hang it up, screw two metal 'eyes' into the board and fasten a piece of strong cord between them.

To start with, whether you plan to make an abstract pattern or a picture, it is a good idea to work out the design first of all on a piece of paper the same size as the board, laying the pebbles in place on the paper, and moving them around until you have found the best arrangement. Then gradually transfer them to the board, sticking them into place with an impact glue. When the adhesive is quite set, fill up the spaces between the pebbles with a grouting mixture, rubbing over the whole surface, after it has dried, to remove any surplus powder.

You can also build up pebble mosaics on jars, tins and boxes, or on waste-paper bins and flower pots. And you can give a new look to an old chest or table by creating mosaics on its surfaces and the fronts of its drawers.

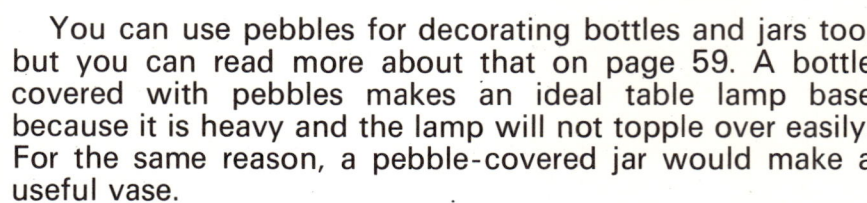

You can use pebbles for decorating bottles and jars too, but you can read more about that on page 59. A bottle covered with pebbles makes an ideal table lamp base because it is heavy and the lamp will not topple over easily. For the same reason, a pebble-covered jar would make a useful vase.

It is quite easy to use your collection to make a pretty framed mirror. Just stick a large square mirror tile on to a larger, square piece of hardboard, arrange a pattern of pebbles around the hardboard edge, and glue them into place.

If you have some tiny coloured pebbles you can turn them into jewellery. This is a simple task if you use the metal jewellery mounts you can buy from a craft shop. All you have to do is stick the pebbles into place. The skill lies in choosing the most attractive shapes and colours for each separate piece.

You might like to create fantastic pebble sculptures by fastening them all over unusually shaped bases. For instance, you could cover a strange rock, or give a twisted log or piece of driftwood a pebble overcoat, to achieve a rough, knobbly effect that is fun to feel as well as look at.

But there is a new popular form of stone-craft that is my favourite, and that is stone-painting. You don't need to be an artist to make some beautiful collectors' items. All you need are some nicely shaped stones about as big as your fist, poster paints, varnish and brushes. Scrub your stones clean, dry them thoroughly, and look at each one to decide what would be the most attractive way to decorate it. You might like to cover it with an abstract pattern, or, if its shape reminds you of something in particular, a frog, or a fish, perhaps, you could paint it to highlight the resemblance. Other stones might make bases for vivid miniature pictures, portraits and scenes.

When you have worked out your designs, paint the stones, let the colour dry, and cover it with a coat of clear varnish. They are now ready to use as ornaments, paper-weights, and doorstops.

You could even organise a stone-painting party competition for your friends, giving prizes for the prettiest, and funniest, results.

Shells

Shells can often be used in the same ways as pebbles.

First, you have to find your shells, recognise them, and prepare them. The most obvious place to look is, of course, on the sea-shore where you will find them in a variety of shapes and sizes. You could also ask friends to bring them home for you from holidays in this country or abroad. Fish-mongers might give you *scallops* and *oyster shells*, and you can buy special and rare ones from a craft shop.

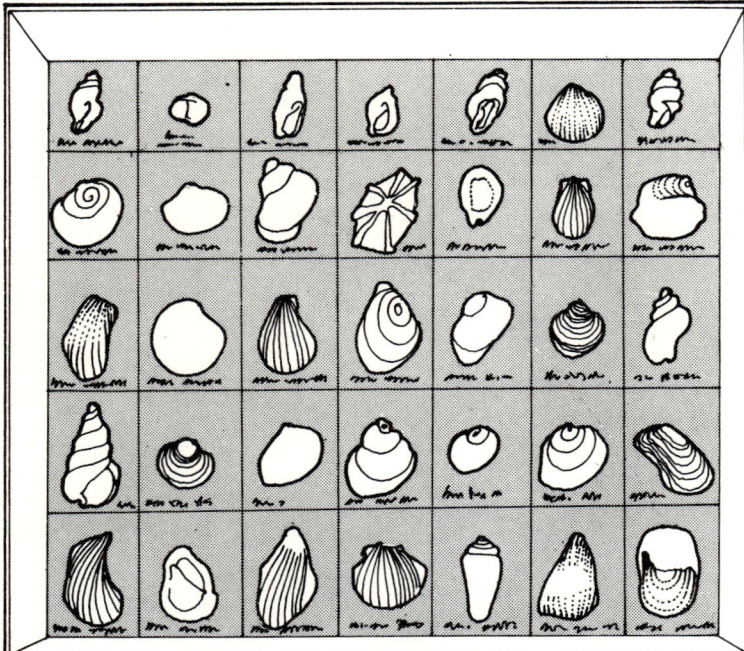

You can make mosaics and sculptures from them. You can decorate pots, umbrella stands, waste-paper baskets, jars, bottles and boxes with them, as well as old furniture. You can use them as an edging for mirrors, picture frames and tea-trays, and there are hosts of new ideas too.

Make sure that your shells are in good condition, and *empty*, then wash them and leave to soak for 24 hours in a solution of 1 dessertspoonful of household bleach in half a bucket of water. Rinse them, dry them, remove any lingering tar stains with turpentine, and your shells are ready for use. Until you start work with them you should store them in boxes, wrapped in tissue or cotton wool so that they don't get scratched or broken.

If you paint your shells with a coat of clear cellulose it will protect them, and preserve their natural colour, but for some jobs you might like to paint them with oils, water paints, poster paints, enamel or lacquer, gold or silver sprays, or nail varnish, taking care not to cover them too thickly in case you hide their delicate texture.

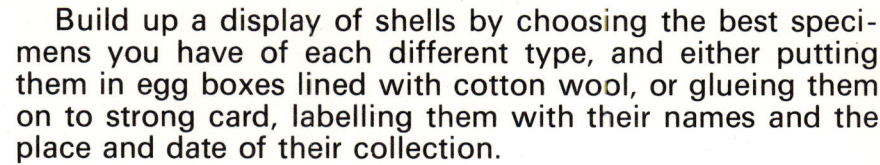

Build up a display of shells by choosing the best specimens you have of each different type, and either putting them in egg boxes lined with cotton wool, or glueing them on to strong card, labelling them with their names and the place and date of their collection.

You can show them off to advantage in a model rock pool. Shape wire netting into the form of a large rock with a hollow in the middle. Dip pieces of muslin into liquid plaster-of-Paris and spread them over the wire until it is all covered. The muslin will set hard and dry in an hour or two and can then be painted to look like a wet rock. Arrange your shells all over it, and stick them into place together with some dried seaweed and a sprinkling of sand.

You would probably enjoy making some of your shells into funny birds and animals. It is quite easy. If you take an oval-shaped *cowrie* shell as a body, two *mussels* for wings, two *carpet shells* for feet, and a small *winkle* for a head . . . Hey presto! You have made a penguin.

A large *whelk*, two tiny *scallops* and a *wentle-trap* can become a bird.

A human figure can be made from an *oyster shell* body, four half *razor shells* for arms and legs, and a *cockle shell* head.

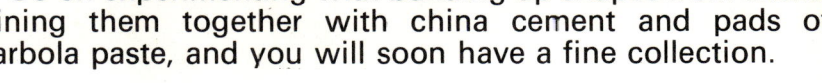

Go on experimenting with building up shapes from shells, joining them together with china cement and pads of Barbola paste, and you will soon have a fine collection.

27

You can make shell brooches by sticking shells on to the jewellery mounts you can buy. Try varying the design by fixing the tiniest ones *inside* big *ormers*.

If you drill holes in your smaller shells you can make necklaces and bracelets by threading them on to nylon or elastic thread.

Some of the larger shells can be used just as they are, as containers. A *conch* or *murex*, for example, can hold arrangements of tiny flowers, or serve as a toothbrush holder on the bathroom shelf. The big *scallops*, *carpet shells* or *limpets* will make unusual pin-cushions if filled with a wad of cotton wool and covered with a scrap of velvet, the edges tucked down and glued to the inside. They can also serve as dishes for butter, jam and sweets, and if they are unpainted, they can be used in the kitchen too. Since they are strong enough to withstand the heat of the oven they can be used for cooking individual egg dishes, or for serving small quantities of hot food.

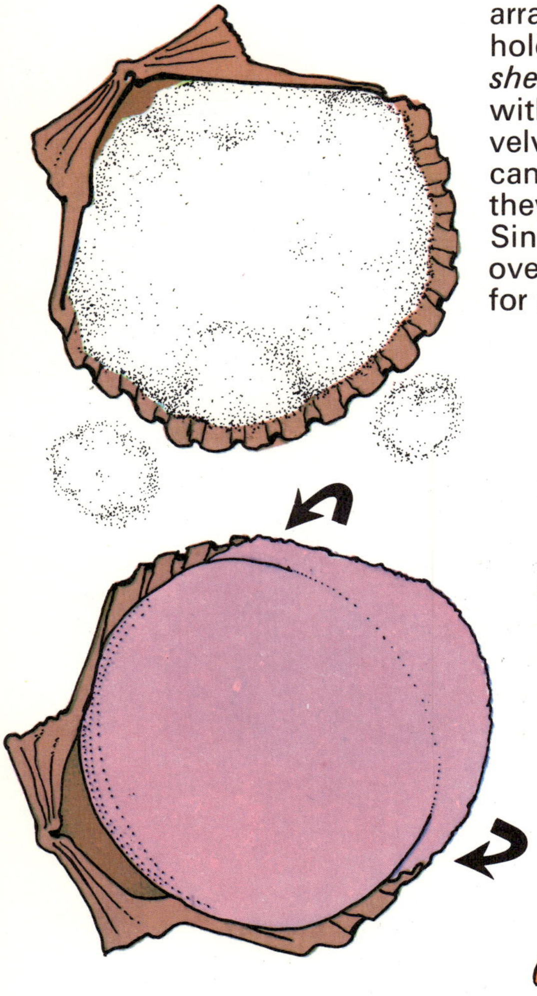

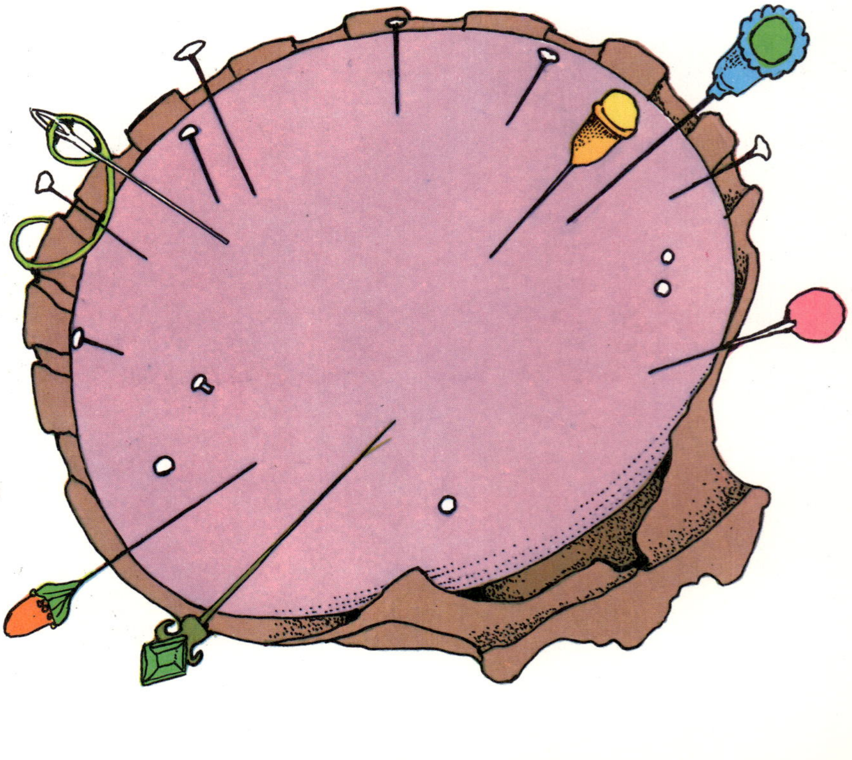

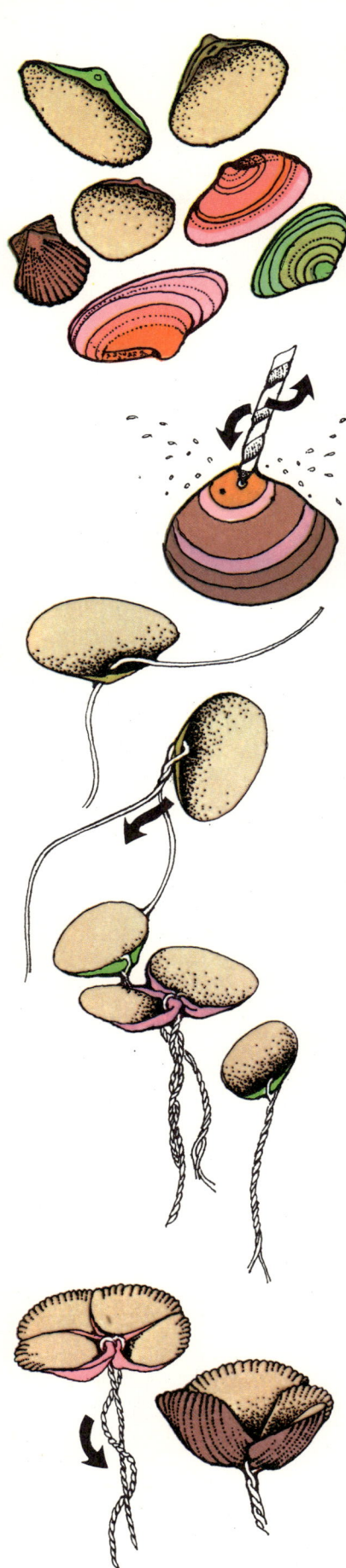

Shell flowers

It is rather more difficult to make shell flowers, but it is worth trying. Choose small petal-like shells, such as little *scallops*, *tellins* or *carpet shells*, and bore a hole through their base with a hand drill. (Practise drilling broken or unwanted shells first, until you get the knack of it.) Thread thin wire through the hole, twisting the two ends tightly together right up to the shell, to make a stalk. Now form the petals into flower groups, winding the stalks together, and fasten the flowers on to twigs picked before their leaf buds have begun to open. Spray the twigs gold or silver, arrange them in a vase, and they will look quite beautiful.

You will find that shells are a most satisfying subject to collect. They are fascinating and beautiful in themselves and they can be used in so many useful and decorative ways. What is more, you will be able to give yourself the splendid name of *conchologist*, or shell collector.

Feathers

Have you ever thought about collecting *feathers*? Some are tiny, some are quite large, but they are all very pretty and there are many things you can make from them.

Look closely at a feather, under a magnifying glass, or a microscope if possible.

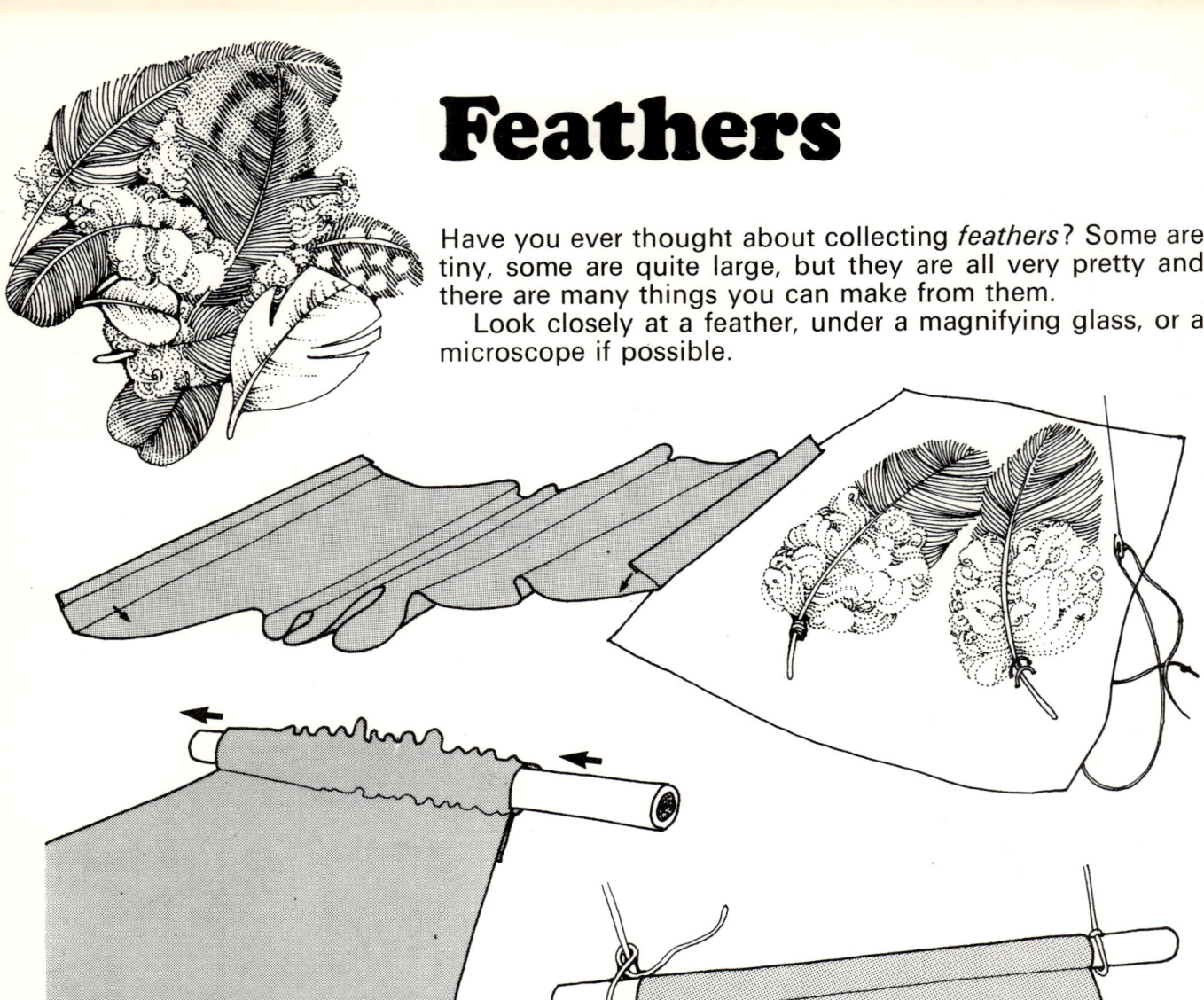

Find your feathers in the places where wild birds choose to live, or where farm and domestic birds are kept. You will find the grey, black and white feathers of seabirds on the shore, or cliffs or sand-dunes. There will be the coloured feathers of water fowl by the edges of rivers and duck-ponds. You may pick up the feathers of other birds in woods or hedges, on moors and mountains, or wherever they nest. Anyone who keeps poultry, or caged birds, will probably be able to give you quite a lot for your collection, or you could ask for them in a pet shop. You might even find them leaking from an old, unwanted cushion or pillow.

I think the best way of displaying the special feathers in your collection is to make a *feather sampler*. Take a piece of strong plain material about 1 yd (1 metre) long, with selvedges at the sides, and sew a wide hem at the top and a narrow one at the bottom. Arrange your feathers on the material, and stitch each one into place by its spiny quill. Push a bamboo cane through the top hem, and fasten a piece of cord to each end so that you can hang it up.

You can glue the feathers on to a large piece of card to make a *feather poster*. Try to find out what sort of bird each feather belonged to and label it with its name, the place it was found, and the date of its collection.

If you have a great many different kinds of feathers you could make a series of posters or samplers, varying the colours of the card or material, keeping one for sea birds, one for cage birds, one for town birds, and so on.

Keep all the feathers left over from your displays because you can use them in many different ways. You can mount the prettiest of the smaller ones between strips of transparent plastic to make bookmarks like those described on page 14.

They can be turned into pretty brooches too. Glue the feathers in a nice arrangement on to a piece of buckram which you have cut to the same size as a brooch mount, then glue them firmly together.

A feather trim can make simple clothes look right for parties. You can sew them on to the hem, cuffs, belt or waistband of a dress; fasten them to a headband or delicate, floating scarf; or attach them to a little fabric handbag.

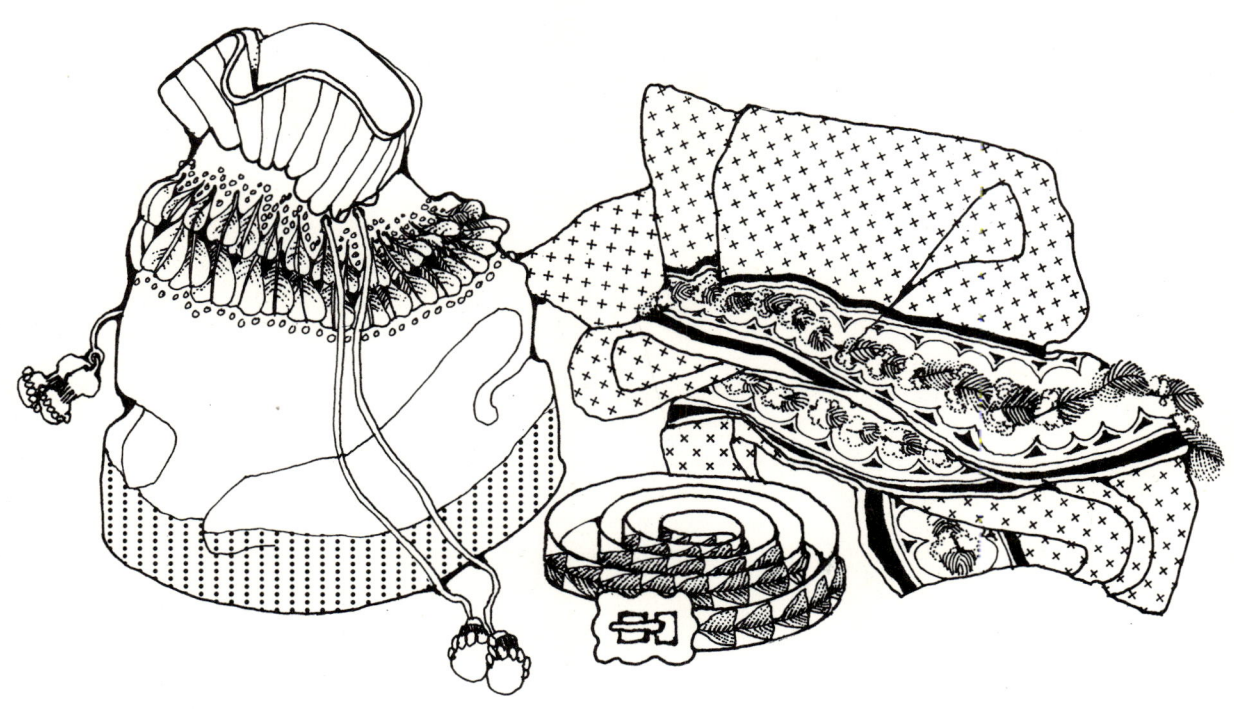

You can use them, like shells and pebbles, to stick on to the lids of jars and boxes to give them a decorative finish — the tiniest ones can be used on the matchboxes described on page 69.

Feathers can be used *with* shells and pebbles to make exciting collages. Feathers of the right size and colour can look like flowers, clothes, trees, smoke and clouds.

It is quite easy to colour feathers. You can dye them by soaking them for a short while in ordinary household dye, before rinsing and drying, or you can paint them with enamel or lacquer. The brightest ones can then be made up into exotic feather flowers.

Start by making a ball of Barbola paste, and glueing it on to the end of a twig. Cut eight feathers into petal shapes, then glue the spiny end of each, in a circle, into the Barbola centre. Arrange a second circle of feathers inside the first, working quickly so that the paste does not get too hard, and finish off by painting the centre yellow.

Feather flowers would make an unusual gift for someone, and there are other gifts you could make too. A feather duster is very simple. Hollow out one end of a bamboo cane to the depth of a finger's length, and squeeze in some glue. Push some long feathers into the centre of this hole, and arrange shorter ones around them until you have a circular shape. Bind adhesive tape around the cane, starting just above the feathers, and continuing until you have covered the stems of the feathers, then wind it back up the cane, and cut it off. Fasten a ribbon loop at the other end of the cane, tying it tightly just below a joint so that it will not slip off.

A painted rectangle of thin wood, with a hole drilled in the top for hanging, can be turned into a jewellery holder. On it, draw the outline of the head and shoulders of an Indian squaw, paint in her eyes and mouth, then stick on thin strands of black wool for her hair. Glue feathers on to the inside of a piece of braid and stick this across the squaw's forehead. Screw in tiny hooks where her ears should be, and put a circle of hooks around her neck. These can hold rings, ear-rings, brooches and beads, and give the squaw a richly bejewelled look at the same time.

A similar board could be painted with the outline of a bird with coloured feathers stuck on for its tail, wings and crest, and a calendar tab glued on at the bottom.

Feathers can be used in your games too. You could make an Indian head-dress for yourself. Fold a strip of paper, long enough to go right round your head, arrange feathers upright inside the fold, glue or staple them into place, then join the ends together. Finish off by painting a vivid geometric pattern on the paper band.

Finally, a party game for your friends. Ask each guest to choose a partner, and give each pair a mirror, a bag of mixed feathers, scissors, a roll of clear sticky tape, and a paper bag big enough to fit on the head of the one who will act as model. Give them a limited amount of time to see which couple can create the most attractive Easter Bonnet by shaping the paper bag, and covering it with feathers, and offer prizes for the funniest, and most attractive, creations.

You see, feathers can be fun.

Bark & Twigs

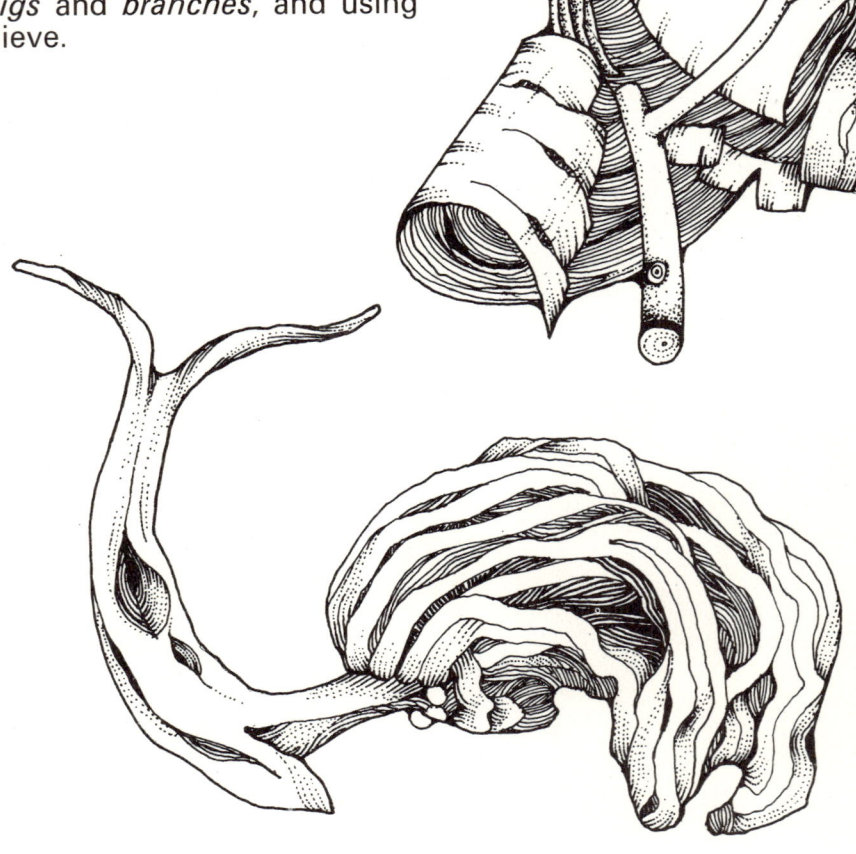

Have you ever picked up a gnarled branch, turned it in your hands, and let the magic of your imagination transform it into a host of strange and wonderful creatures? A simple piece of wood can look like a snake, a toad, a dragon, a prehistoric animal, a moon monster. You can have great fun making a collection of *twigs* and *branches*, and using them in this game of make-believe.

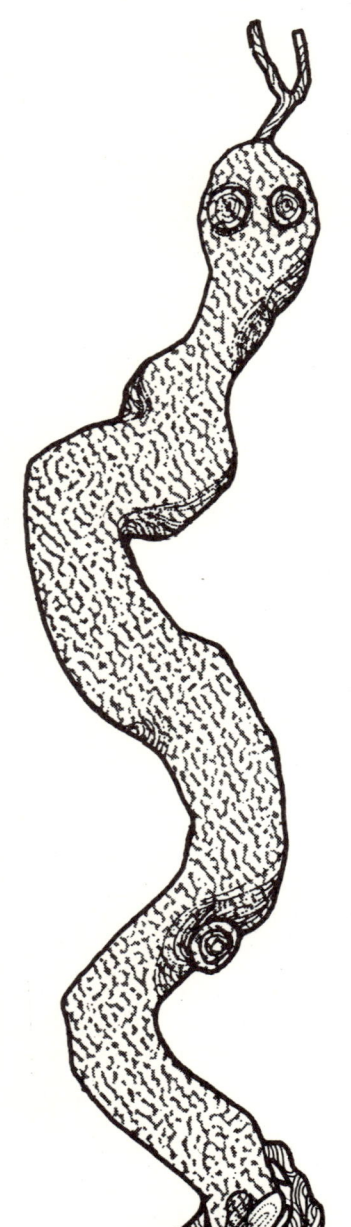

You will find branches lying around wherever there are trees, or you can pick up smooth, sea-washed drift wood on the beach. Hunt around until you find some interesting pieces that set your imagination working, make sure that they are not rotten or infested, then carry them home for your collection.

It can be an interesting hobby to high-light the likeness you see in the branch by adding one or two details. For instance, if it looks a *bit* like a snake to start with, you could stick on two shiny button eyes, add a tiny, twiggy forked tongue, and paint V-shaped snake-markings on its back to make it look *very* like a snake. Then hang it from your ceiling by threads and it will look as if it is wriggling in the draught.

Now see what other strange animals you can conjure into life. If you like, you can stick or screw branches together to get more realistic effects, giving the illusion of legs, or long knobbly necks.

Dinosaurium

If you have an old aquarium you can turn it into a *dinosaurium* by putting in a collection of small, stick dinosaurs. Fill the bottom of the aquarium with sand, arrange rocks on it, and old, stunted pieces of wood, some upright, others lying on the sand, and group the dinosaurs among them as realistically as you can. You might like to paint a background landscape and stand it behind the aquarium. This idea could also work with moon monsters in their own, strange moonscape.

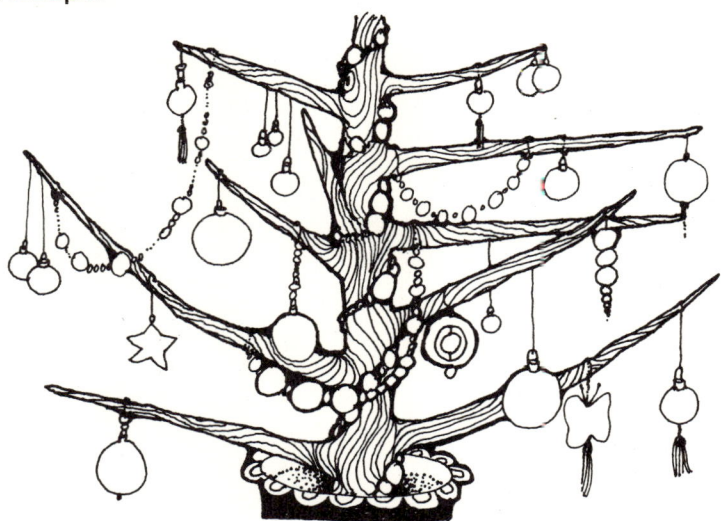

Though some branches and twigs are interesting because they remind you of something else, others are interesting in their own right, just because they are beautiful or unusual. You could try fastening one or more of these to a white-painted board, and hanging it up as a collage, or joining them together with wood screws or glue to make a wood sculpture. A coat of clear varnish will protect them, and make them shine.

A graceful branch, sprayed silver, and pushed firmly into a bucket of sand, will serve as a lovely Christmas tree when hung with glass baubles and beads.

Your collection could make unusual Christmas presents too. You could transform a branch into a smart key-rack by varnishing it, screwing small hooks in a row along it, and fastening a cord to both ends so that it can be hung up. If you use larger, straight hooks, it could be used as a tie-rack instead.

A thin piece cut off a thick branch would make a useful teapot stand, with small pieces glued underneath to make feet.

You can even make cards and gift-wrapping paper from bark rubbings, but you can read more about that on page 39.

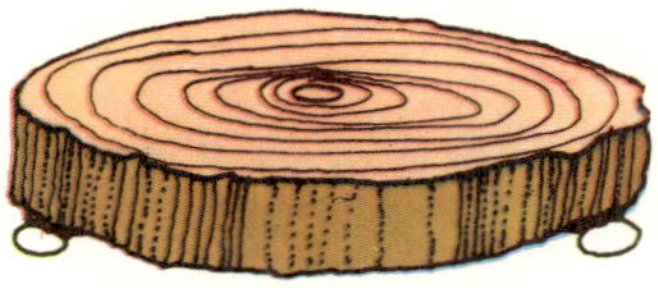

If you are careful with your hands, and have learnt how to use a penknife properly, you could teach yourself to whittle. Start by practising on a small branch. Strip off the bark, then, with the point of your knife, cut out shapes of diamonds and circles until you have covered it all over with a rich, textured pattern. Finish by giving it a coat of gloss paint or varnish to protect it, and emphasise the carving. Once you have mastered the skill you will be able to make more complicated designs, using flower and feather shapes, crosses and curls.

You might be able to see examples of whittled wood if you look in rural craft shops and country museums, where there are often whittled walking sticks, shepherds' crooks, and crosses on display.

I think you will be surprised at how much beauty can be created from wood.

Rubbings

In the section about leaves we described how to make a 'scribble print' which is a type of *rubbing*.

A rubbing can be made from any object which has a raised or indented surface. Try it for yourself now. Take a coin, lay it flat, cover it with a piece of thin, plain paper, and slowly and carefully rub a soft pencil or crayon over the top, always moving it in the same direction. Soon you will see the pattern on the surface of the coin transferring itself on to the paper.

Now collect together a simple rubbing kit and look around the house to see what else you can find to make up a collection of rubbings. You will need shelf paper, lining paper or printers' off-cuts, a set of stubby wax crayons, either black or coloured, a duster, to clean the object before you rub it, and tape and scissors, to fasten the paper into place if you wish to have both your hands free.

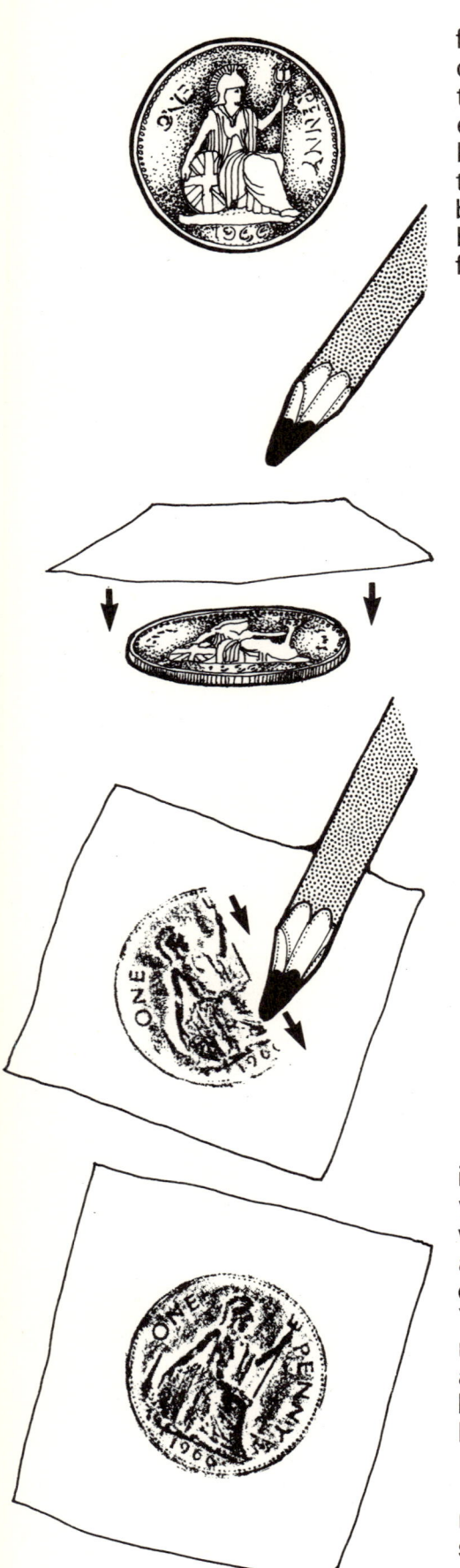

You will be surprised at the number of objects you can find that will make excellent rubbings. Here is a list of some of the things you might find at home: textured wallpaper; the names stamped on cutlery; a mosaic teapot stand; engraved copper table mats; the printing on a hard-back book binding; the brass key-hole surround on a desk or door; the dimpled glass in the bathroom window; some patterned buttons; the name disc on a dog's collar; embossed leather book marks; ceramic coffee-table tiles; and textured vinyl floor tiles. See what you can collect together on your list.

You could spend a busy rainy day making rubbings indoors, but on a fine day you should go out and see what you can find in the streets, in the park, or countryside. You will discover lots of things to keep you occupied. Drain and coal-hole covers, and water hydrant lids are good objects to start with, as well as the markings on lamp posts. You might find a mile-stone or sign-post which has the right sort of surface for rubbing. Besides these, a lot of houses and shops have suitable name plates or raised numbers, but of course you must always ask permission of the owners before you set to work.

Some walls have a knobbly surface texture that will reproduce in a very interesting way, and you will find the same applies to bark rubbings which come up in fascinating patterns, every sort of tree being quite different.

You might like to make a collection of your most successful rubbings by putting them together in a large, loose-leaf file or folio, labelling each one on the back with information about where and when it was rubbed. This could make an interesting dossier of your environment, and will cause a lot of curiosity and surprise among your friends who will begin to see their own neighbourhood with new eyes.

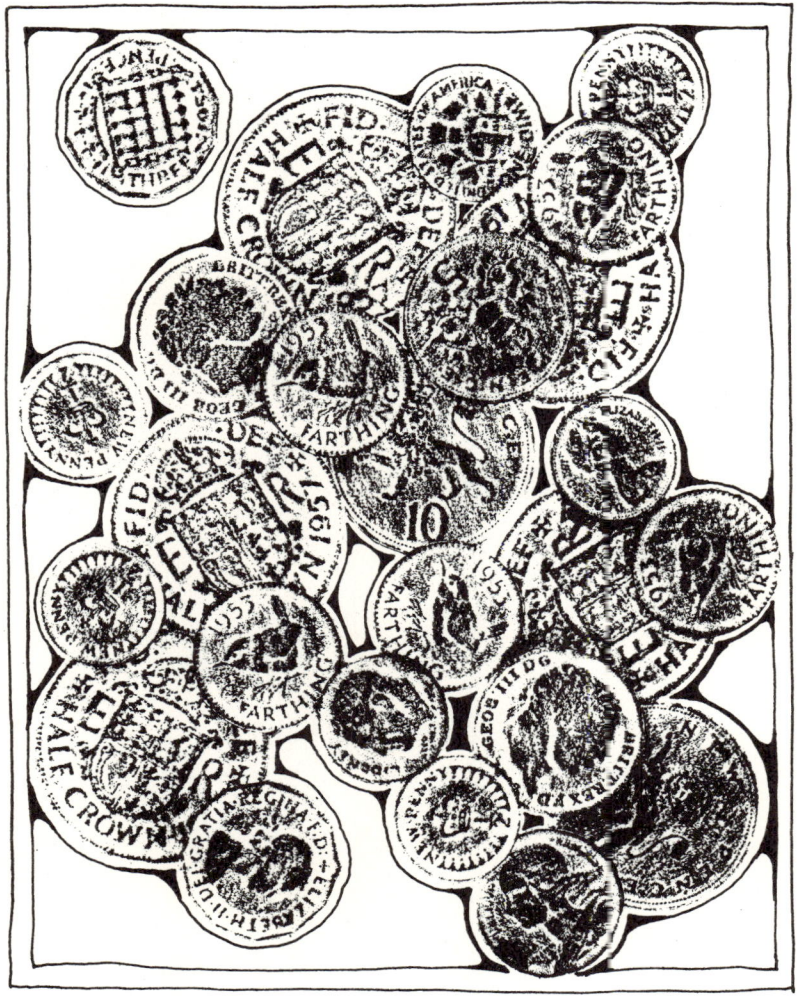

When you have had some practice and are producing very neat coin rubbings you can make an unusual picture by grouping several together on one sheet of paper, arranging them in an attractive pattern, some of them overlapping each other. Then stick the paper on card, and glue a neat edging around it.

Large, coloured bark rubbings can make very smart gift-wrapping paper, and the prettiest of your small ones can be cut out and stuck on to pieces of card to make individual greetings cards, book-marks or table-setting place-names.

Other rubbings can be mounted, either singly or in groups, to make posters and framed pictures for your walls.

If you become interested and expert in the technique, you might like to go on to the absorbing hobby of church brass rubbing. The method is very similar, but you will need rather more sophisticated equipment; cobbler's wax, or 'heelball', instead of crayon, and architects' detail paper instead of your lining paper, which is rather narrow and tends to yellow in time.

You must also ask the vicar's permission, and be prepared for the fact that he will probably charge a fee, though this is often reduced for young people.

A black rubbing, or one in silver or gold, cut out and mounted on a piece of red card, with a ribbon slotted through holes punched in the top, and a calendar tab fixed at the bottom, would make a lovely Christmas gift.

You can use your craft as the basis for a treasure-hunt-with-a-difference, which can be great fun. Plan out a route around your neighbourhood, and walk along it, taking rubbings of items that you come across on your journey. You will need to make several copies of each rubbing, one for each couple who will be joining in the game. Number the rubbings in order, write a helpful clue on the back, then hand them over to the competitors, asking them to find their way around the route in a limited time, and return with details of where each rubbing was made. The prize goes to the pair with the highest number of correct answers.

Buttons

Nearly every household has its button box. There always seem to be buttons to spare, because the clothes they have belonged to usually wear out long before the buttons themselves.

Nowadays we take buttons for granted, and it's difficult to imagine a time when people didn't button up their coats and shirts, but, in fact, the history of buttons does not go very far back in time.

If you like the idea of making a collection of buttons you could start with a button project and discover their story. Begin by asking yourself these questions. Who were the first people to use buttons? What were early buttons made from? Were the first buttons used to fasten things together? If not, what were they used for? How did people fasten their clothes before they began using buttons? How are the buttonholes made?

Trace the progress of buttons to the present day, and then consider other modern methods of fastening. Perhaps one day buttons will have fallen out of use and future generations will know about them only as strange antiques, like flat irons or quill pens.

Look for information about buttons in your local library, or school library, in history books, encyclopaedias, and in reference books about costume through the ages. Museums are good places for finding out, too, and art galleries where there are old portraits on view. Here is a clue to start you searching in the right period of time. In Shakespeare's play, *King Lear*, the dying king's last wish was 'Pray you, undo this button.'

When you have found out all you can about the history of buttons you could write an account of it in a loose-leaf scrap book, adding dates, quotations, illustrations, and, wherever possible, buttons themselves, fastened to the pages in little transparent envelopes. Finish off by designing a bright, attractive cover for your Button Book, building up a collage of buttons, and sticking them firmly into place on paper; or sew them on to a cloth cover.

If you hunt through junk shops, and get into the habit of haunting jumble sales and markets, you will probably find some good old buttons, and sometimes you will see them advertised for sale in the sort of magazines that specialise in items of interest to collectors.

You might like to concentrate on just one or two particular types of buttons, collecting only the Hunt buttons, presented to members of established packs, for instance, or Service buttons. Many of the uniforms of the Armed Forces are equipped with specially designed buttons, and the ones dating from the eighteenth and nineteenth centuries are particularly interesting and valuable. But civilian uniforms, like those of the police, transport workers, post office officials, Salvation Army and some youth groups, have their own distinctive designs too.

You could specialise in modern decorative buttons, which are often very beautiful and unusual, and can be bought reasonably cheaply in shops or craft centres. If you are clever with your hands, you might like to design your own. Buy large, flat, plain buttons, and either paint miniature pictures on them or coat them with a thin film of transparent glue and stick on tiny beads, shells, pasta, seeds, sand or fish gravel. If you wish you can then spray them with colour or give them a coat of glitter dust. You never know, they could become collectors' items of the future!

Paint and varnish the buttons on an old coat to brighten it up.

Since buttons are designed to be sewn on to cloth, the best way to display them is to make a button sampler, like the feather sampler for which you will find directions on page 30. You can vary this idea by arranging the buttons on the material to make up an amusing picture, adding any extra details with a few simple lines of stitching. Birds, cats, pigs and people can all be easily conjured up, and if you experiment you will be able to think up many more possibilities.

Buttons were not always used as fastenings; sometimes they were for decoration only, and they can be used in exactly the same way today. For instance, they can be sewn round a collar or cuff, on a belt, pocket or epaulette, or made into an edging round a hem, down the seaming of a skirt, or the outside of a sleeve. You can make an unusual scatter pattern on a pair of plain curtains, or a bedspread.

If they are smooth-backed buttons they will stick on to flat surfaces quite easily, so they can be treated in the same way as shells or pebbles, built up into patterns on plain boxes, on the lids of screw-top jars, or stuck all over a plant pot as shown on page 24.

You might like to thread the prettiest ones on to strong cotton, or elastic thread, to make necklaces or bracelets . . . and a very special group of matching buttons can be glued on to jewellery mounts to make an unusual set of ear-clips and brooch.

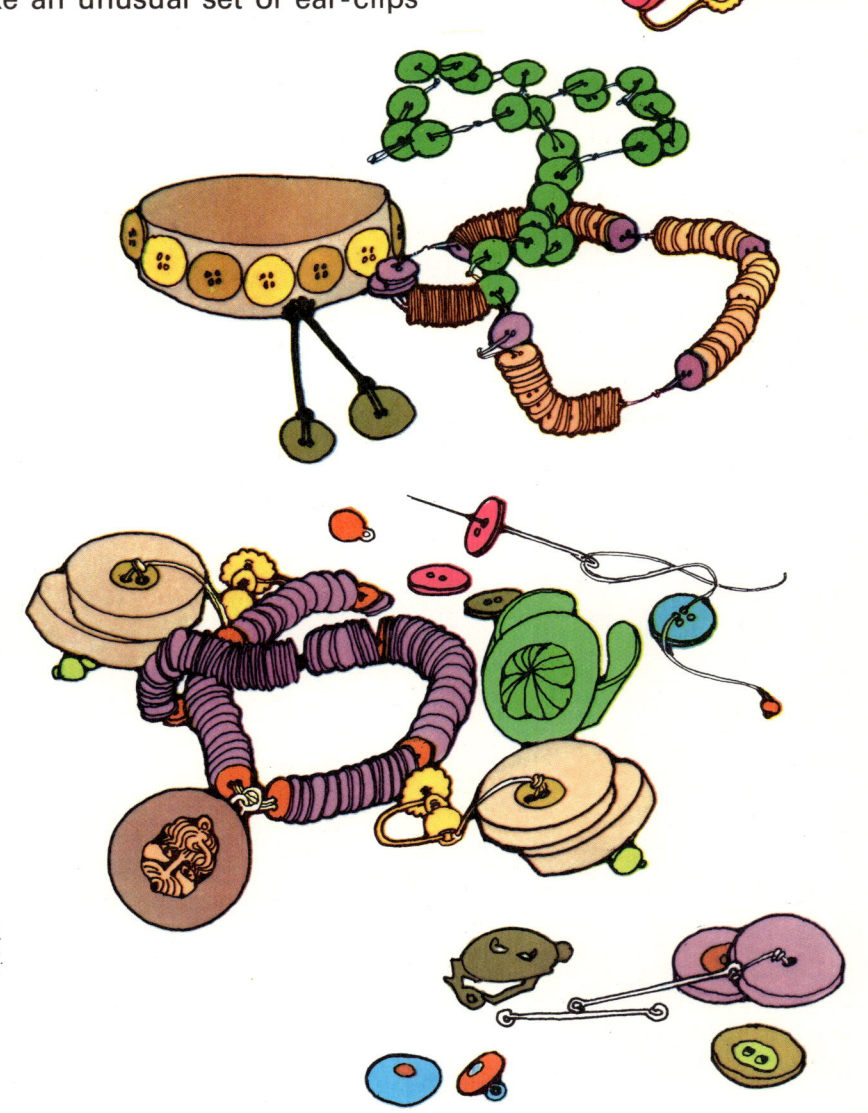

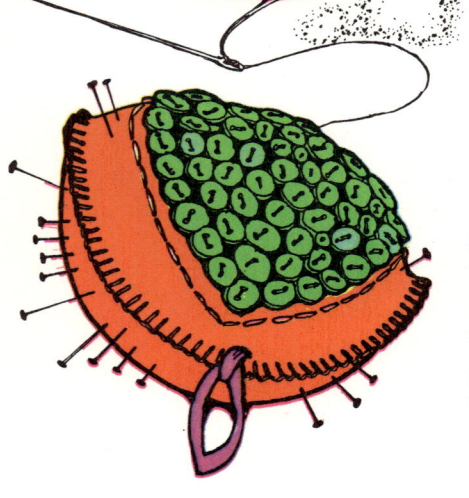

This would make a pretty and individual gift, and so would a buttoned pin cushion. You need two small circles of felt, some wadding for the stuffing, and coloured silks. Make a button picture, such as an animal, bird, or funny face, on one of the felt pieces. Sew each one into position when you have decided exactly where it should go, then stitch on any extra details with embroidery silk. Now sew the two circles together, one on top of the other, with blanket stitch, pushing the wadding inside before you complete the last two inches. Finish off securely, add a ribbon loop for hanging, and the pin cushion is complete.

Abacus

Why not use some of your spare buttons to make a counting frame for one of the younger members of the family?

Paint a cardboard shoe-box inside and out with bright poster paint, and leave it to dry.

Stand it up on one short end, and measure the long side into eleven equal sections, marking these off with pencilled crosses half way between the back, and the front, open end.

Thread a needle with a very long piece of strong nylon thread which has been firmly knotted at the end, and push it into the inside of the box from the outside, where you have made the topmost mark. Thread on one button, using the sort which has holes right through, push the needle out through the other side of the box, then down and into the inside again through the second mark. Thread on two buttons, then take the needle back across the box, and out of the mark at the other side.

Carry on down the length of the box in this way, putting on one extra button for every row, until you get to the bottom row, which will have ten buttons. Then fasten off the thread tightly, knotting it on the outside of the box.

In this way your button collection will give hours of pleasure, and help, to children just beginning to learn about numbers.

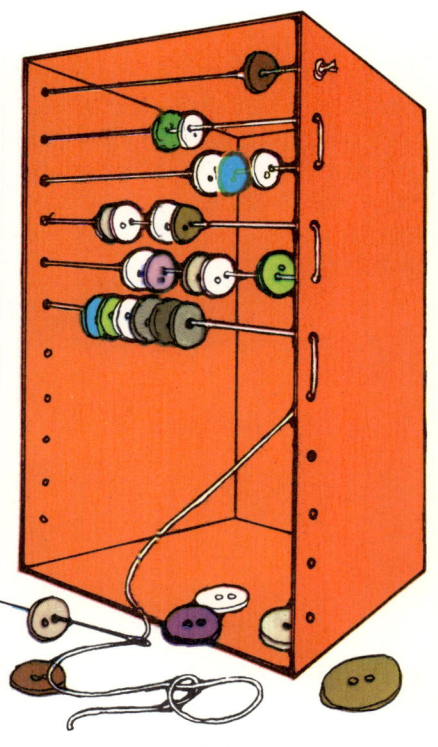

Match together the buttons that you find, in colour, shape or size, and keep them together in sets, in little transparent envelopes or small plastic bags. They will be very useful as spare counters in games such as ludo, tiddleywinks, or games of your own invention.

Don't be surprised if other members of the family come looking for buttons in your collection that they can 'borrow' to sew on their clothes. They will value your collection almost as highly as you do, but for a different reason.

Keys

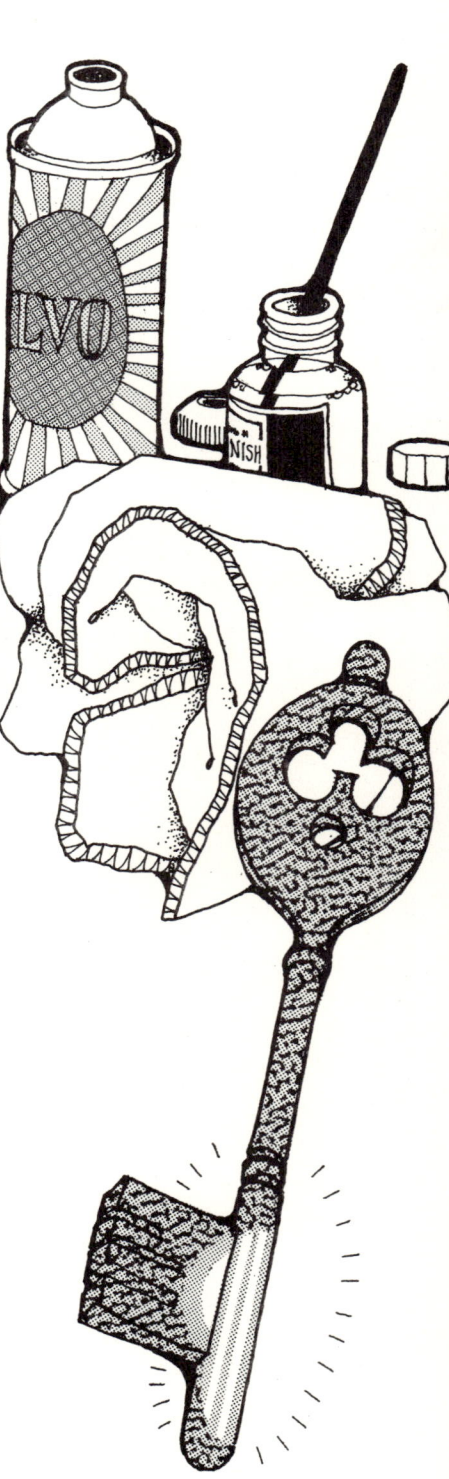

As a collectors' item, *keys* are in many ways similar to *buttons.* They, too, are used to fasten things together. They, too, can be plain or very decorative. They, too, are historic – but their history reaches back much further into the past. You will probably be able to see a real Roman key in a museum, but I doubt whether you will ever find a Roman button.

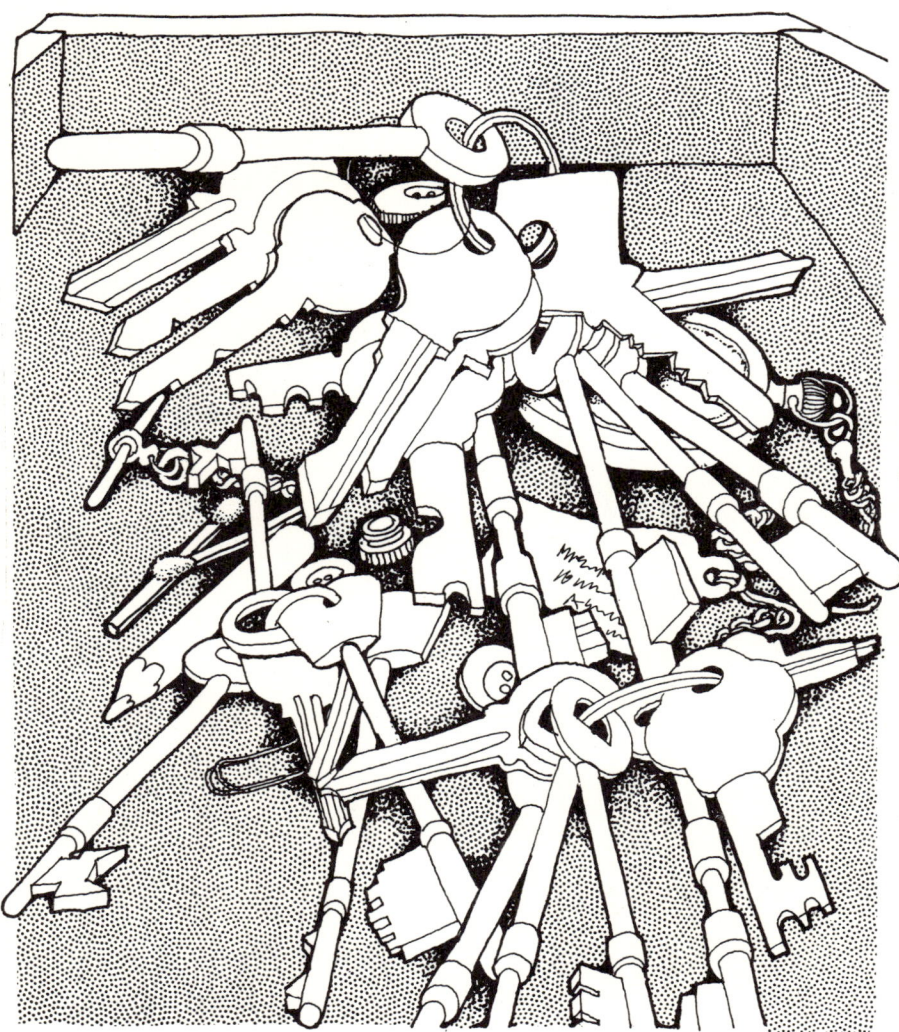

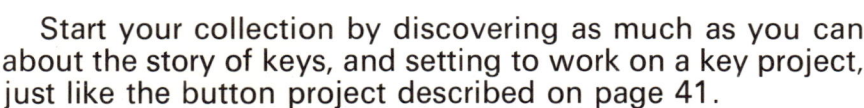

Start your collection by discovering as much as you can about the story of keys, and setting to work on a key project, just like the button project described on page 41.

You will find many junk shops have drawers and boxes full of old keys which will cost you very little, and you will be able to get rather more special items, at rather more special prices, in some antique shops. There are old, unused and unwanted keys lying around in most households as well, and often people will be only too glad to give them away.

When you acquire a new key for your collection, clean it up with metal polish, and give it a coat of clear varnish to keep it shiny. Then try to work out approximately how old it is, what metal it is made from, and what it was originally used for. It might have locked a door, a drawer, a case, a padlock, a piano, a musical box ... there are so many different possibilities. Write the information on to a twist-on label, add the date and place of its collection, and fasten it to the key's shank.

To display your best keys you could sew them on to hessian, or stick them to card. But I think a better way, since it takes up much less room, is to thread them on to coloured cord and hang them, either vertically or horizontally, against your walls. Thread the cord through the 'eyes' of the keys, and keep them well-spaced and held into position by knotting it securely.

A mobile made from keys, arranged so that they collide as they spin round, would make a musical ringing sound.

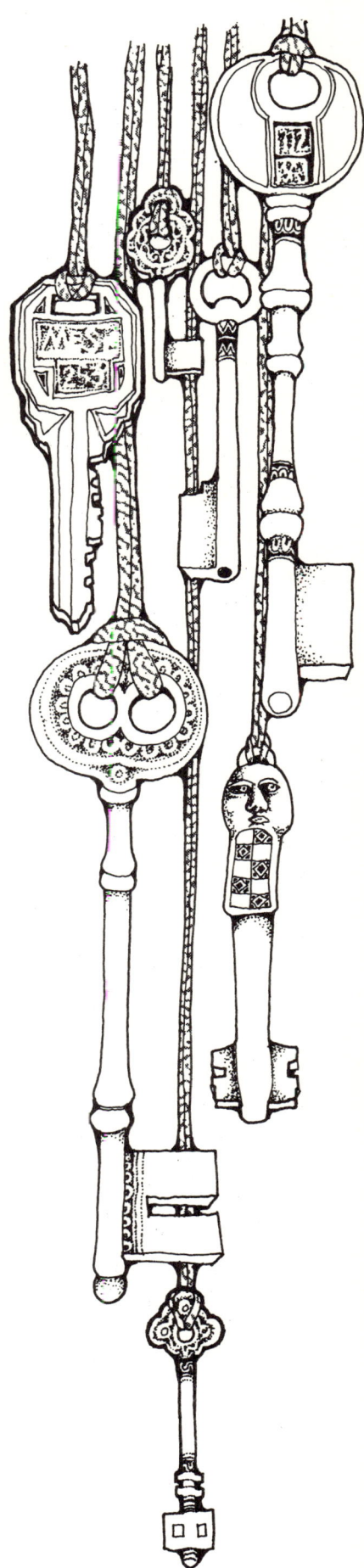

Since keys have such very interesting shapes, you can use your spare ones in many decorative ways. For instance, they will make up into splendid pieces of jewellery. Knotted together on a leather thong to form a pendant they will look like the old-fashioned *chatelaines* that housekeepers used to carry fastened to their belts.

Tiny bunches can be looped on to plain hoop ear-rings with twists of fine wire. They can also be hung on to a chain bracelet, belt or necklace, or glued lengthways on to a simple tie-pin.

Try sticking a circle of keys to a broad webbing belt, to the epaulettes, waistband or pockets of a battledress jacket. Or arrange them in a pattern on a handbag, or duffel-bag, or satchel. Sew them on with a few stitches through the key-ring hole, and they will flap up and down in an attractive way.

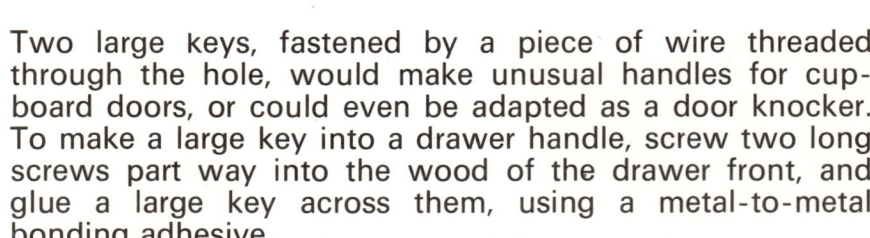

Two large keys, fastened by a piece of wire threaded through the hole, would make unusual handles for cupboard doors, or could even be adapted as a door knocker. To make a large key into a drawer handle, screw two long screws part way into the wood of the drawer front, and glue a large key across them, using a metal-to-metal bonding adhesive.

Use your keys as a stencil to make interesting shapes and patterns. Lay them on a sheet of paper in an unusual pattern and draw around them. Paint the pattern in bright colours. in the same way they can be used to mark motifs on a dress or tee-shirt. When you have drawn round the key, embroider round the outline, or fill in the middle with fancy embroidery stitches.

With a little care, keys can be built up into fascinating, unusual pictures or sculptures. Cover a piece of hardboard with black velvet, sticking it down firmly round the edges at the back. Arrange shiny silver keys on this background and fasten them into position with tiny blobs of transparent glue to make either an attractive abstract pattern or a representational picture. You will soon notice how some of the more rounded key-shapes can look like bodies, while the longer, thinner ones remind you of legs and feet, and the more you move them around, the more ideas will spring to mind. You should find it easy to make a monster with wide open jaws and lots of sharp teeth.

To make a 3-dimensional key sculpture you will need to stick your keys together with an epoxy resin glue. Have some idea in your head of the final shape you want to create – it might be based on a circle, a pyramid, a wheel or a box – and go on adding one key to another, glueing them wherever they touch, until you have made the right effect. If you have trouble in holding the keys together until the adhesive has set, form your shape over a support made of clay, then wash this away when they are firmly fastened. Spray them with silver or gold paint.

Keep the sculpture quite small and you will be able to use it as a table ornament. You will be surprised to see how much pleasure people will take in simply picking it up, feeling it, and turning it and twisting it in their hands.

Picture Postcards

Nowadays we expect to see *picture postcards* for sale wherever we go on holiday and we enjoy sending them home to our friends.

But they have not always been part of the holiday scene. The earliest ones began to appear in shops, hotels, railway bookstalls and restaurants less than a hundred years ago. Ever since then, they have been extraordinarily popular as souvenirs, or for writing brief letters. Many remain intact after all these years, and can be easily and cheaply collected.

The popularity of the picture postcard was at its highest between 1890 and 1915. They poured out from the printing presses in enormous variety, including view cards, portraits, greetings, advertisements and jokes, and when the First World War broke out they had their place on the battle field too, being sent home by the soldiers to their wives and sweethearts, carrying with them photographs and messages of love.

If you hunt carefully in junk shops, collectors' shops, and second-hand book shops you might be able to collect some of these special early examples. Look for silk postcards, war souvenirs, recruiting cards, and some of the earliest of Donald McGill's funny seaside cards. You might also find that friends and relatives have old treasures tucked away in desk drawers, scrap-books and photograph albums.

Of course, some of the postcards being produced today will also become of historic value if they are kept in good condition for long enough. Those which celebrate a special occasion will be sought after by the social historians of the future, so keep your eyes open for picture postcards which celebrate a royal wedding or birth, a landing on the moon, the first flight of an important aircraft . . . or other events which make up part of life in the twentieth century.

There are so many different sorts of postcards, that it's a good idea to specialise in just one or two types if you are building a collection. You might like to concentrate on map cards, joke cards, bird and animal cards, art reproduction cards, or views of places you have visited at home or abroad.

You can display them in an album, or stack them upright in a shoe-box, covered with wallpaper and decorated on the outside with surplus cards.

They can be hung up in pairs, fastened back to back on coloured ribbons pinned to the ceiling.

You might be able to make a whole wall mural by covering it from floor to ceiling and side to side with a collage of postcards, fastened on in a way which will not damage the paint or paper.

A smaller collage can be built up on a piece of cardboard and mounted in a picture frame. Try making an arrangement on a tray or trolley, or on the top of a table, chest or desk. Cover them with a sheet of plate glass or thick, transparent adhesive vinyl, and this will protect them.

You can transform a set of cards into matching table mats quite easily if you follow the instructions given on page 14, in the section about wild flowers. Put four cards together for each mat, grouping similar scenes together.

If your speciality is view cards you might like to make a pictorial map from them. Take a large piece of heavy cartridge paper and draw in the middle of it the outline of the country your cards come from. Mark all the places represented in your collection with dots, and print their names beside them. Then fasten one end of a narrow coloured ribbon to each dot and lead the other end to the border around the map. Stick it into place with a blob of glue and fix a postcard beside it.

Eventually your whole border will be filled up with colourful pictures. You could cut little details from any left-over postcards and place them on the map itself, and you will be able to see at a glance what the country looks like.

If you have some old postcards of a place, try to find pictures of it as it looks today. Put them side by side to show up the difference between the old and the new.

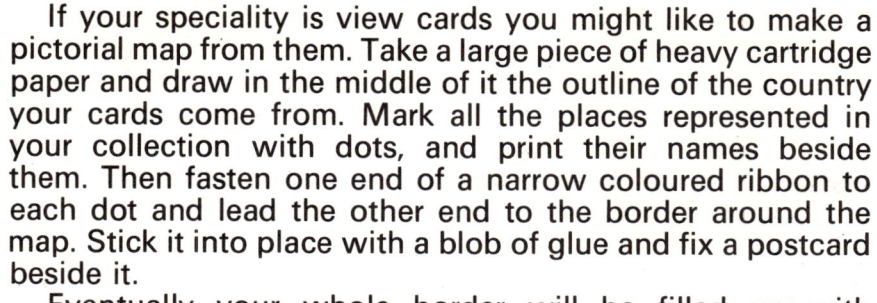

Look at the stamps on old postcards before you stick them down on to anything; they might be worth collecting too.

No matter what sort of cards you collect and how you display them you will probably have some left over. Why not cut these up to make gay scraps which have all sorts of uses? For instance, you could make them up into scrap-books for yourself, your friends, or the children's ward of the local hospital. You could transform them into greetings cards, calendars and bookmarks. You could stick them to plain paper to make dust covers for your books. You could decorate a dull wastepaper basket . . . and you could work out a dozen more ideas of your own.

So, the next time the postman pops a picture postcard through your door, don't let it get thrown away – collect it.

Autographs

If you are interested in celebrities from any sphere – show business, the world of sport, or politics – you might find it a very exciting business to collect their *autographs*.

The most interesting way is to try to contact them personally. Wait at the stage door for an actor or entertainer, stand near the dressing room if you are waiting for your favourite footballer, go to a big political meeting it it's an M.P.'s handwriting you want to collect . . . and eventually you will come face to face with the celebrity himself. Few will refuse you their signature if you ask for it pleasantly and offer them something to write *on* and *with*. Never take it for granted that they will be carrying a pen of their own. It is up to you to offer one.

Collect the majority of your signatures in a loose-leaf pocket book which you should always carry with you in case you meet a famous person by chance.

It can also be fun to build up a collection of autographed programmes, either of sporting fixtures or theatrical events. A programme giving details of a Yehudi Menuhin concert, for instance, signed by Menuhin himself, is of greater interest, and value, than a plain piece of paper with his name written on it. If you manage to collect a lot of autographed programmes sort them out into their separate sections, keeping one for athletics programmes, one for football, plays, concerts, and so on, and file them. You could decorate the cover with copies of autographs which you have traced from the originals. Trace them directly on to the cover, or on to pieces of paper which can be mounted as a collage.

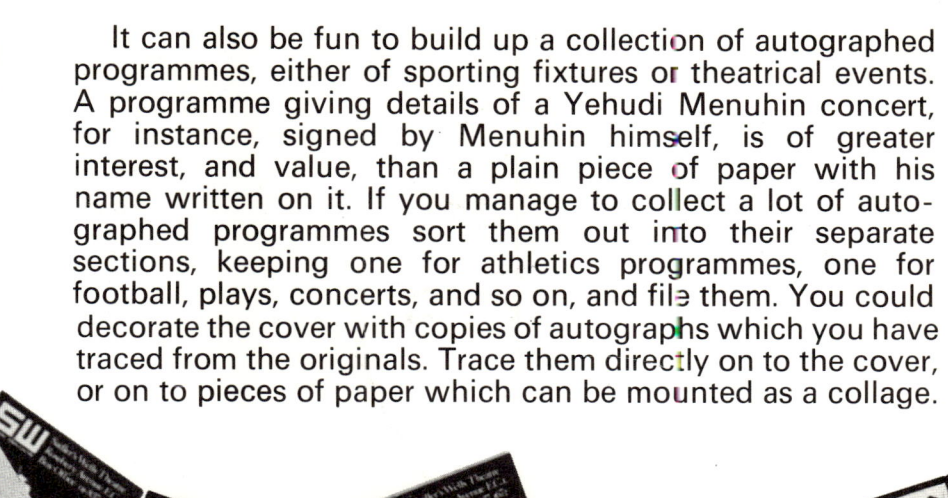

Perhaps you would like to make a collection of autograph letters from famous people. This is not as difficult as you might imagine. Often if you write a pleasant sensible letter to a person you admire, showing that you take an interest in his work and achievements, and enclosing a stamped addressed envelope, he will send you a reply, and even if it has been typed by a secretary it will almost certainly have his signature on the bottom.

In fact, many celebrities such as pop singers, disc jockeys, film stars, TV personalities, will go one better and send you a signed photograph. These, like the letters, can be mounted in an album, and you can write beside them brief details of the personality's life and career.

To make sure your letter reaches the personality of your choice, write to him at the place where he is currently working, addressing letters to a television or radio company, film studio, football club headquarters or theatre, for example, and they will almost certainly be forwarded to him at his home address. Don't be too impatient, it may be quite a long time before you get a reply, especially if the person you have written to travels a lot.

When you have collected your autographs you will probably want to display them. You can show people your pocket books, files and albums, of course, and you might like to frame some of your most interesting signatures, letters and photographs. But you can also use them in several decorative ways if you make tracings of the originals and transfer them to other surfaces. You could copy them on to a plain cloth, bedspread or tee-shirt and then embroider over them in fine chain stitch, using a different colour for each different name. If you did this on a tea towel you could then hang it up to make an unusual wall decoration.

It is also possible to transfer autographs on to china. Make a tracing of the writing in the usual way then, laying the paper on a thick pad of newspaper, prick tiny holes along it. Now hold the pricked autograph against the surface you want to decorate and paint over it, using a fine brush dipped in enamel or, preferably, one of the new paint tubes, rather like pencils, that you can buy in art shops nowadays. Lift off the paper carefully, and you should find a dotted paint line beneath. All you need to do is join the dots together with a little more paint. In this way you could decorate a whole tea-set with the autographs of the famous.

So far we have been concerned with celebrity names. But sometimes it is nice to collect the autographs of friends, especially if you tend to move house quite often and do not want to forget them. Either a hospitality table-cloth, or a friendship or holiday book, make ideal souvenirs.

The cloth is covered with embroidered autographs in exactly the same way as described above, except that there is no need to trace them. Using a soft pencil, your friends can sign their names straight on to the material when they visit you.

The friendship book is kept for the autographs of the people who visit your home; the holiday book for those you meet when you are away. Before you part, ask them to sign their names, and the date, and perhaps to add some comment or quotation. You will find these will give you many vivid and happy memories as time passes.

Bottles

Bottles play a very important part in our lives because so many of the things we use are often packed and sold in them. Think of milk, and medicine, for instance; shampoo and scent; beer, and bath oil; whisky and wine . . . the list is very long.

Bottles have been in use for thousands of years. The earliest ones were probably made from animal skins, but glass bottles were found in the ruins of Pompeii. The Ancient Egyptians used glass too, but they also had bottles made of stone, alabaster, bronze, silver and gold. Now, though we still use bottles of glass, and sometimes of stone, and metal, they are also made from plastic and polythene. New *synthetic* materials are being developed all the time and we may soon have bottles and containers made of these.

You might like the idea of becoming a bottle-collector. Many antique shops sell old ones, but these may be rather expensive, so look for them instead in junk shops and jumble sales, and ask relatives and friends to see if they have any lurking at the back of their cupboards. Among the most interesting of the old bottles are those with seals impressed on them, carrying the initials, coat of arms or crest either of a private individual, or a factory or merchant.

Look for medicine bottles with the chemist's name pressed into the glass, and also for bottles made of hand-made glass, or stone.

The first thing you must do when you acquire a new bottle is to clean it thoroughly, especially inside. Never taste any liquid left in it, it might be poisonous.

Modern bottles are worth collecting too. Some wine firms are still making lovely sealed bottles. Others are plain, but beautifully shaped. And there are special novelty bottles produced as souvenirs and gifts, as well as a whole range of pretty miniatures.

Those that have corks or stoppers can be useful about the house. I use a Portuguese wine bottle, which has a little handle, for vinegar. A stone Dutch Genever bottle stands on the bathroom shelf filled with bath salts, and a chunky, sealed brandy bottle often holds one or two branches, or some dried grasses.

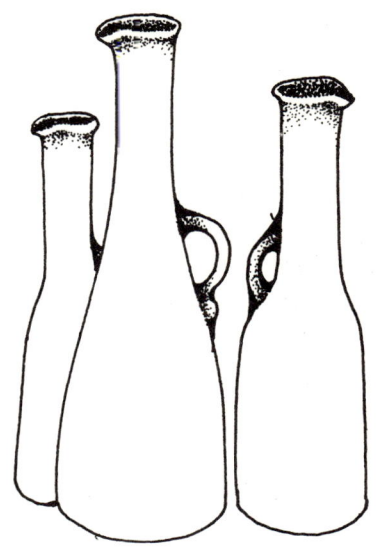

Transparent bottles can look attractive if you fill them with shells, marbles or coloured pebbles, and use them either as candle-sticks or table lamp bases. Most electrical shops will be able to provide you with a special adaptor, then all you will need to finish the job is a bulb and a lamp shade.

There are lots of different ways you can decorate the outside of a bottle. For instance, you can stick on a covering of varnished shells, or small, bright pebbles. You can apply a mosaic of the tiny pieces of coloured glass, pottery or plastic, or even sticky paper, that you will find in your craft shop. Or you can paint it, using enamel or gloss paints.

It can be great fun to make a bottle family by painting them to look like people. Choose a tall thin bottle for Mr Bottle, a smaller, rounder one for Mrs Bottle, and a miniature for Miss Betty Bottle. Their corks can be decorated as hats. Stick a feather in Mrs Bottle's, and add little rims of stiff paper to turn Mr Bottle's into a trilby, and Betty's into a panama. Then, using a very fine brush, paint faces on the necks of the bottles, and clothes and arms on to the flasks. If you like you can add strands of wool for hair, and give Mr Bottle a moustache.

Or what about making a fantastic fish from a Chianti bottle? Turn it on its side, and imagine its rounded base as the fish's head, and its neck as the tail. Cover it all over with scraps of coloured paper cut into diamonds to look like scales. Then cut out a large fin and stick it along the top of the fish's back, and two smaller ones to go at either side of its head. Finish off with two round goggling paper eyes, and a ribbon streamer tail fastened round the cork. Fix a cord at either end of the bottle, and hang it up.

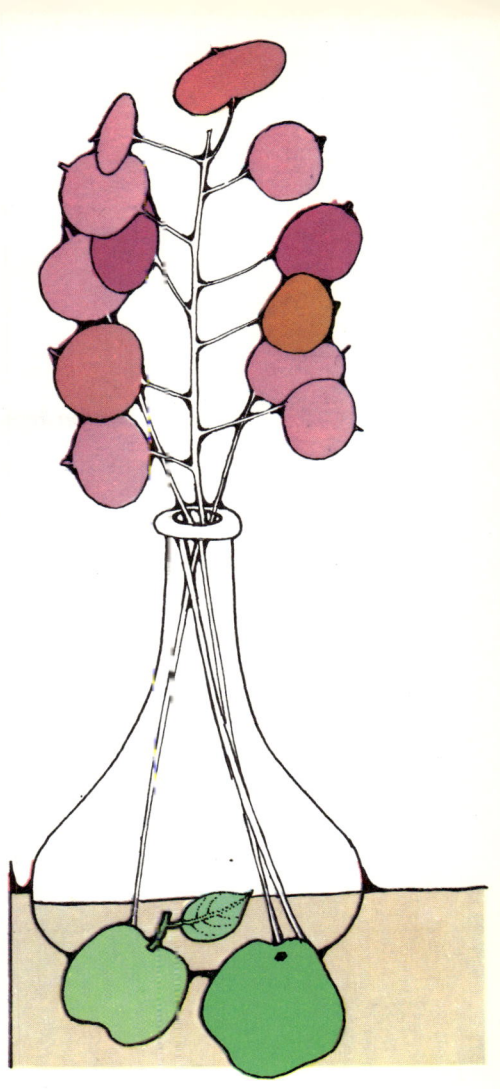

You can display your bottles handsomely by standing them in groups on a shelf or room-divider, having filled the clear ones with coloured water. This will look particularly effective with a light shining from behind them.

You can even make a set of musical chimes if you have eight bottles, all exactly the same shape and size. Leave one empty, and pour water into the other seven so that each one contains a little more water than the last. The seventh bottle should not be much more than half full. Play the chimes by tapping the bottles with a pencil and they will give you a complete musical scale. You will get the same effect by blowing across the top of the bottles with your lips, or with the hose of a vacuum cleaner, switched to blow instead of suck.

Advertisements

Most of us come across *advertisements* in one form or another practically every day. They appear in papers, magazines and comics; on television; on carrier bags and wrapping paper; we see them on hoardings and in shop windows. They are part of our modern way of life.

If you are interested in making a collection of modern advertisements you might like to begin by finding out the story of advertising through the ages. Write it up in a notebook, and add illustrations and examples whenever you can. Remember that public criers' calls, sign boards over shops, and symbols, like the barber's pole and the pawnbroker's three gilded balls, were all advertisements in their own way.

If you can find any very old magazines and newspapers you'll see that their advertisements often have a strangely quaint look about them, and are very different from the ones we are used to today. Advertisers have always tended to display their products against a background which shows the current fashions in clothes, furnishings, cars and colours.

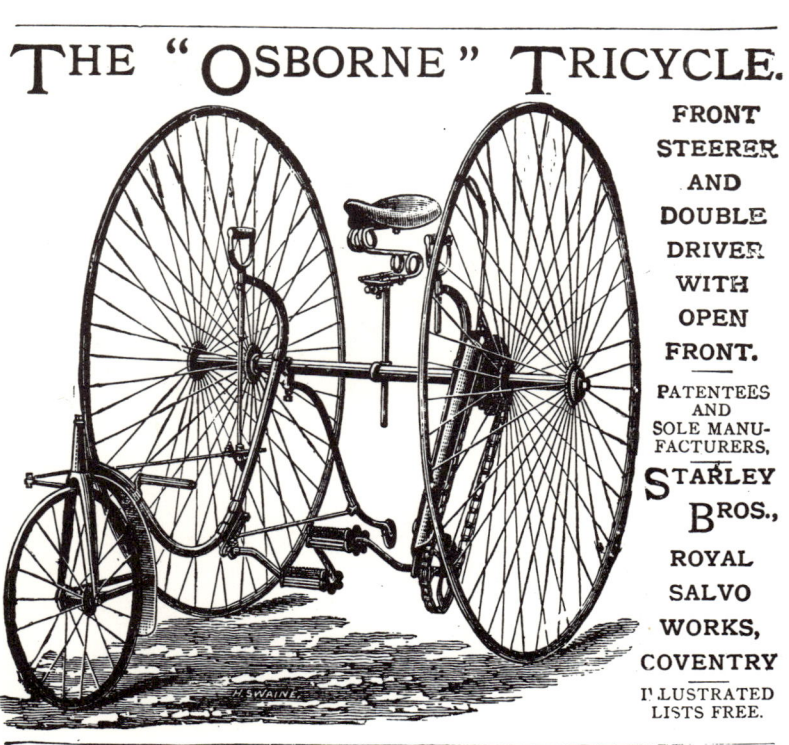

THE "OSBORNE" TRICYCLE.

FRONT STEERER AND DOUBLE DRIVER WITH OPEN FRONT.

PATENTEES AND SOLE MANUFACTURERS, STARLEY BROS., ROYAL SALVO WORKS, COVENTRY

ILLUSTRATED LISTS FREE.

To make a collection of contemporary advertisements you need first to decide on some sort of plan or theme, so that you can be selective. For instance, you might choose one particular product, a fizzy drink, perhaps, or a type of bicycle, or a brand of chocolate, which you think is well advertised, and collect the whole series of advertisements which promote it.

Collect advertisements which reflect one of your hobbies. I have a young friend who is a keen music an. He discovered that notes of music and musical terms cropped up in a whole variety of advertisements, and now has a collection which shows how music was used to boost the sales of beer, winter coats, jewellery, handbags, sweets and soft drinks, among other things. History enthusiasts might like to look out for advertising campaigns which use historical characters or events, animal lovers will discover that domestic pets feature strongly in attempts to persuade people to buy, and sportsmen will find that advertisers frequently use team games, athletics, or sportsmen to help sell their product.

If you have a tape-recorder you can add sound advertisements to your collection of visual advertisements by taping them from commercial radio or television; some are very funny, some are even beautiful. Be sure to label and date the recordings carefully. In the future they will be a very interesting taste of what life was like in the seventies.

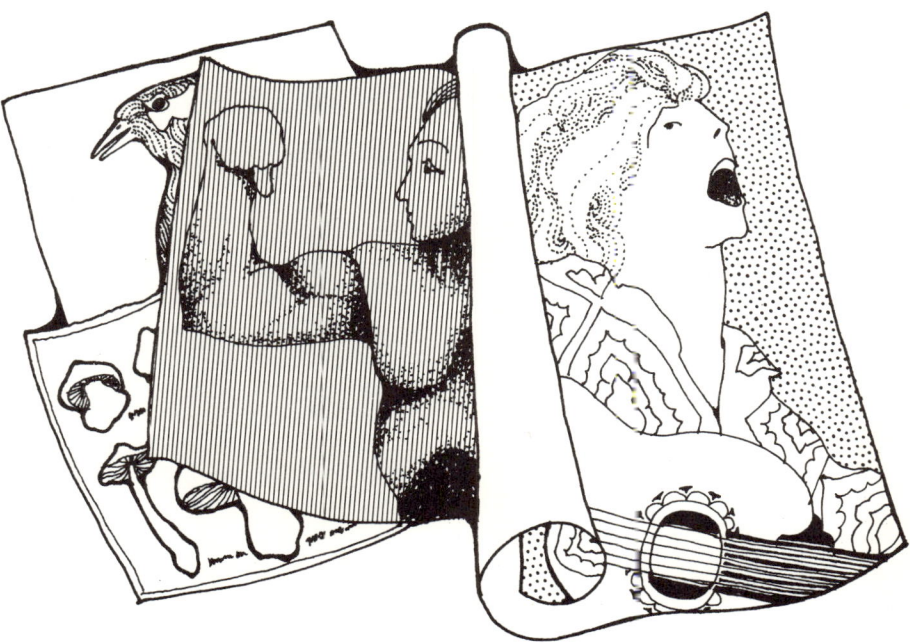

There are lots of ways you can display your press advertisements. The simplest is to paste them into a loose-leaf scrap-book, adding details of the date and the publication from which they were collected.

But since modern advertisements are often very decorative you might prefer to use them in an ornamental way. You could make a huge mural across a bedroom wall, sticking them on in a way which does not damage paint or paper. On a smaller scale they could be made up into an interesting collage on a plain waste-paper basket, lamp-shade, table-top or tray, provided that they are given a protective coating of clear varnish, or covered with transparent vinyl sheeting. A series of small advertisements could be used to make an unusual set of table mats, following the method outlined on page 14 for flower mats.

Tickets

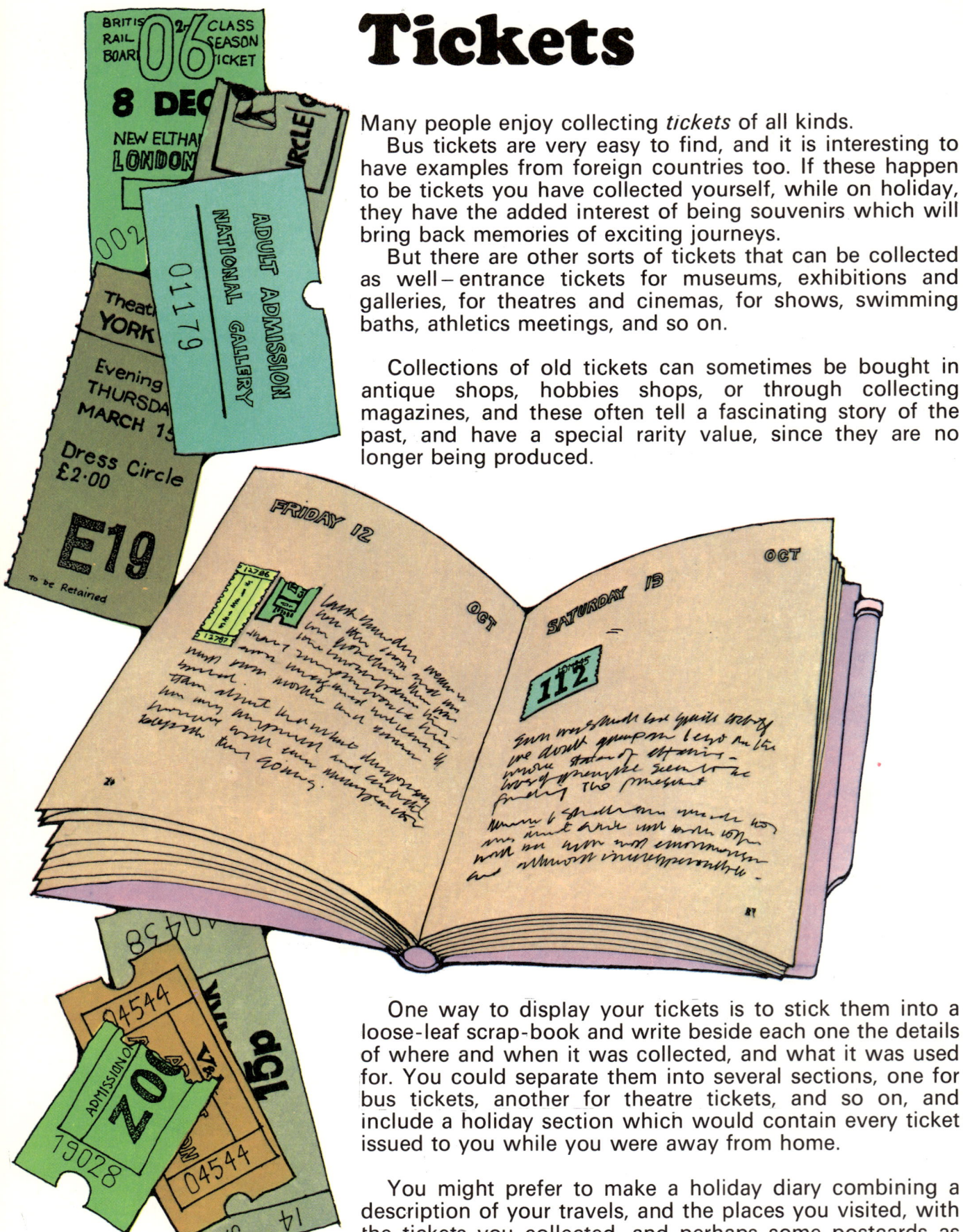

Many people enjoy collecting *tickets* of all kinds.

Bus tickets are very easy to find, and it is interesting to have examples from foreign countries too. If these happen to be tickets you have collected yourself, while on holiday, they have the added interest of being souvenirs which will bring back memories of exciting journeys.

But there are other sorts of tickets that can be collected as well – entrance tickets for museums, exhibitions and galleries, for theatres and cinemas, for shows, swimming baths, athletics meetings, and so on.

Collections of old tickets can sometimes be bought in antique shops, hobbies shops, or through collecting magazines, and these often tell a fascinating story of the past, and have a special rarity value, since they are no longer being produced.

One way to display your tickets is to stick them into a loose-leaf scrap-book and write beside each one the details of where and when it was collected, and what it was used for. You could separate them into several sections, one for bus tickets, another for theatre tickets, and so on, and include a holiday section which would contain every ticket issued to you while you were away from home.

You might prefer to make a holiday diary combining a description of your travels, and the places you visited, with the tickets you collected, and perhaps some postcards as illustrations.

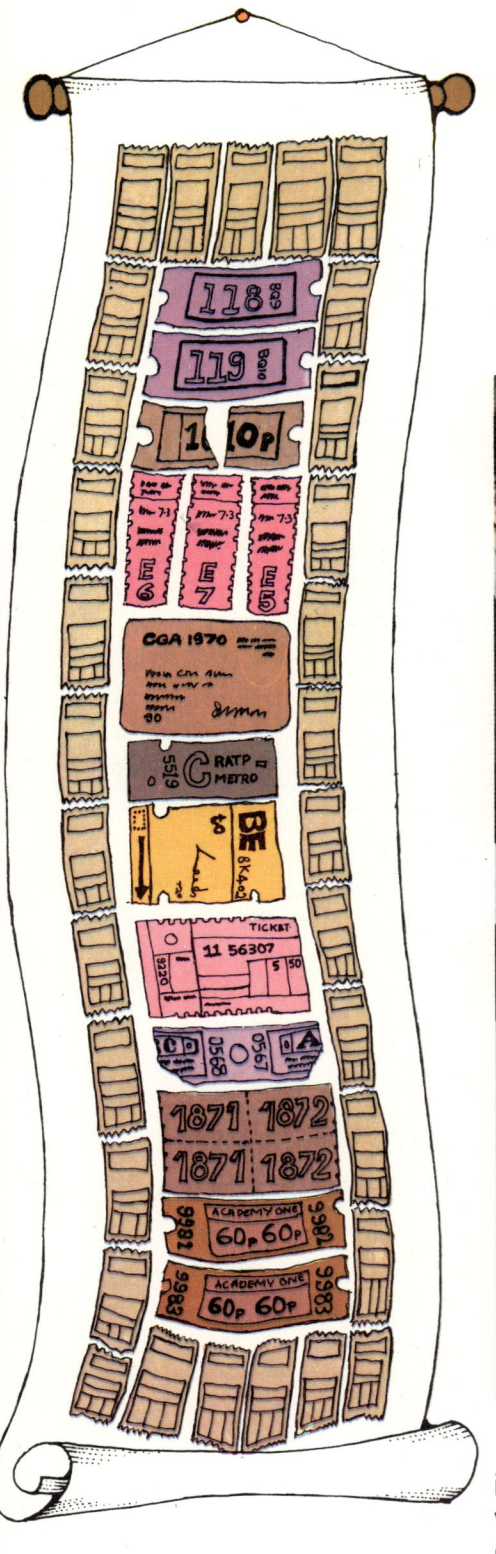

Even when you have used part of your collection of bus tickets for a scrap-book, diary or map, you are bound to have a lot left over. Some could be used for a travel game of your own. Cover a large board with numbered squares, leaving one or two as hazards, such as *'Your bus breaks down. Go back twelve squares,* and rewards, such as *Your bus has had new tyres fitted – take another turn.* Shuffle your tickets and use them as playing cards which allow you to move the same number of squares as the price, or part of the date, printed on them. This is just a general outline of the way the game could be played. You will get the most fun from it if you work out the rules and details to suit your own ideas.

A decorative collage can be made from tickets, perhaps including scraps of timetables and programmes to add to its visual variety and texture. All you need is a large rectangle of heavy paper or thin card. Cover the entire surface by pasting on all the material you want to use, laying some of it sideways or upside down, and varying the colours as much as possible. You will be surprised to see how gay this will look when it is finished, and has pride of place hanging on your bedroom wall.

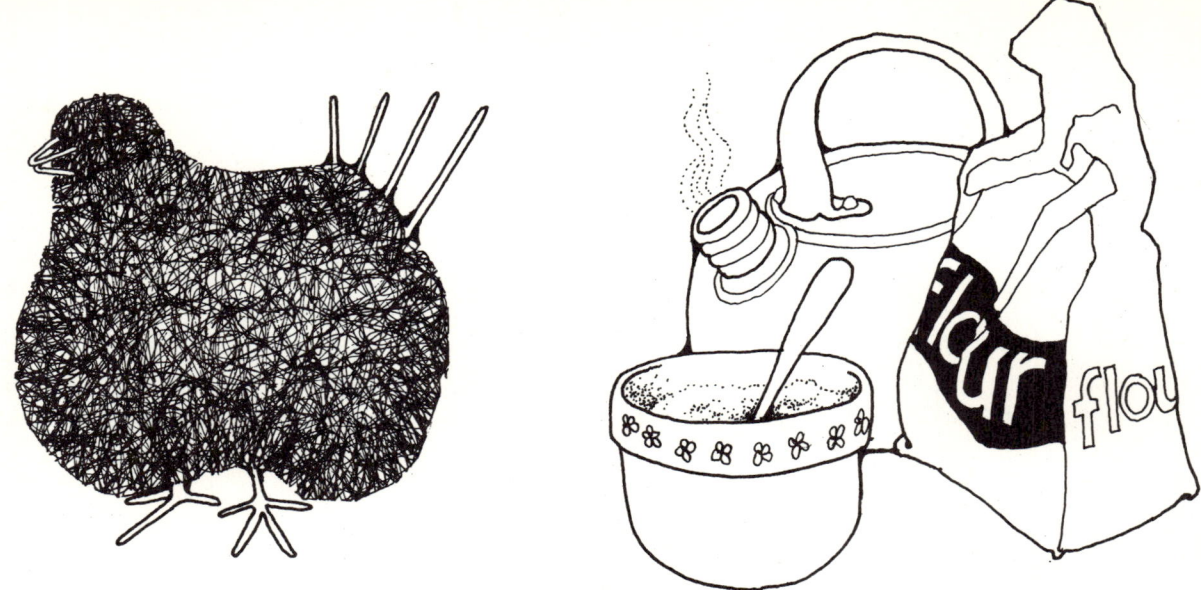

Finally, you might like to try papier mâché modelling with your tickets. This can be a fascinating hobby. Begin by making a basic form from chicken wire, which can easily be squashed into the shape you want, a simple bird or animal would be quite good to start with. You can use either a patent wallpaper paste which can be bought at most hardware or decorating shops, or make your own flour and water paste which is better and cheaper, but more trouble. Pour boiling water on to flour to make a stiff mixture, stir it vigorously, then add enough warm water to turn it into the right sort of creamy consistency to brush on easily. Now build up on the wire form, layer upon layer of strips of newspaper coated with paste until it is the shape you want, and finish with a thick outer covering of the most decorative and interesting tickets in your collection. When it has completely dried out paint the figure with a coating of clear varnish, and it will remain a colourful and unusual item in your ticket collection.

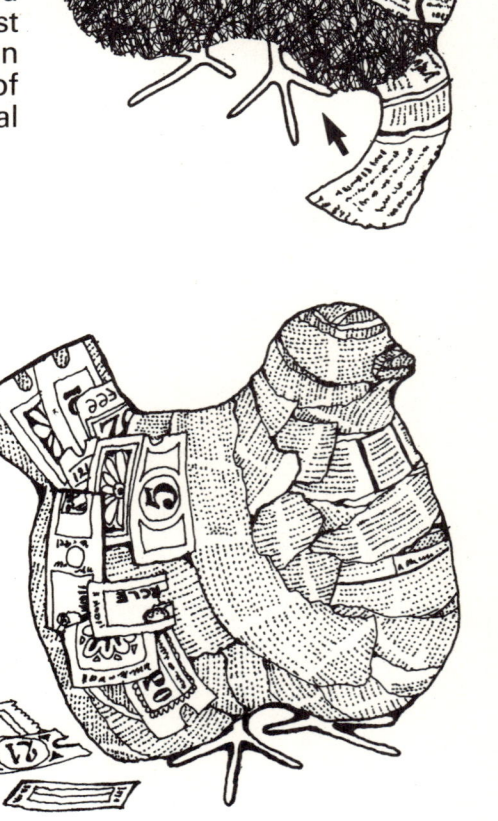

Matchboxes

A lot of people find *matchboxes* and *booklets* are ideal things to collect since they are small and light, plentiful, cheap, and available in a great variety of attractive and interesting designs.

If you too would like to become a *phillumenist*, start by collecting examples of all the common matchboxes most frequently used, then look for special advertising boxes and booklets, such as those which are sometimes presented to customers by hotels and restaurants, as well as gift and souvenir packs. If you go abroad, or have friends who travel a lot, you will be able to make some interesting foreign additions to your collection. And if you are very lucky you might be able to find some old examples, rare now, which were in circulation many years ago.

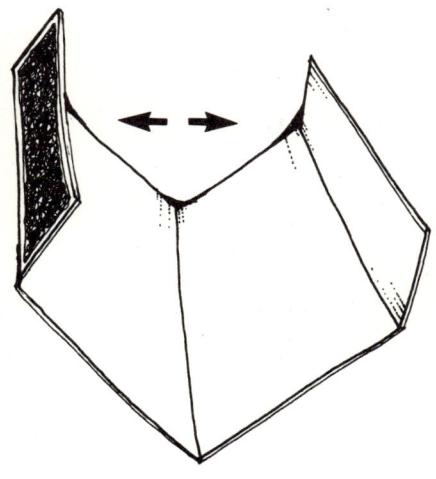

You could keep your matchboxes in a shallow drawer or cardboard box, but if you want to display them you should throw away the box itself, and use only the cover. Cut along one edge so that it can be unfolded into a flat rectangle with all its faces visible at the same time. This can then be fastened on to a large rectangle of rigid card, and neatly labelled. It is a good idea to have several of these display boards, and group different categories together. You might like to keep one for match booklets, another for foreign matchbox covers, another for souvenir covers, and so on.

If you are planning to use some of your collection for decoration, you need only part of your matchbox covers, perhaps the most attractive side cut from each one. Collect them together to make up a kaleidoscope pattern on the surface of a plain box or tin, the front of a drawer, a door panel or window sill. Simply stick them into place, and cover with a coating of clear varnish to protect them and keep their colours bright.

Matchboxes left over after you have made up your displays can be used in several ways. For instance, stuck together, and either painted, or covered with scraps of material, they can be made up into a whole range of doll's house furniture. Chests of drawers, sofas, armchairs, beds, coffee tables, room-dividers and storage systems can easily be designed from matchboxes either used complete, or separated into box and cover.

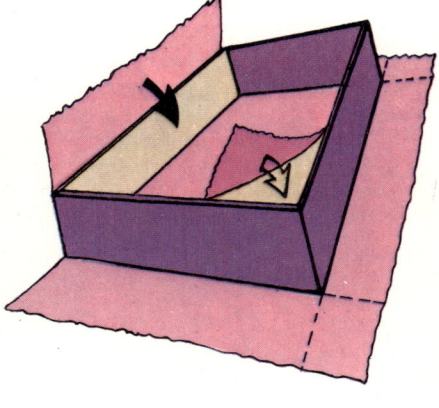

A matchbox cover can also be used as a printing device, for making patterned papers and cards. You can either leave the cover in its original shape so that the edges of the open end form a rectangle, or you can bend it to make different shapes, like those shown.

Charge the edges with water-colour paint, and press carefully on a sheet of lining paper, using the different shapes and a variety of colours to make an interesting all-over pattern.

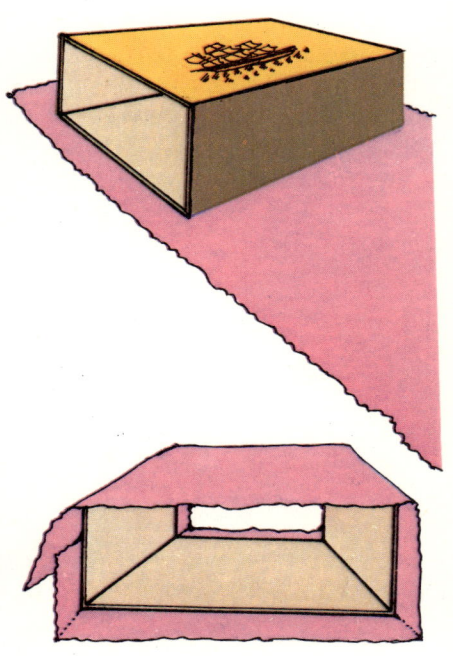

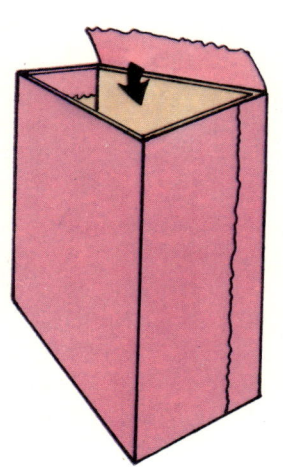

My own favourite method of using up spare matchboxes is to decorate them in such a beautiful way that they become collectors' items in themselves. The fact that they are tiny and fragile makes them all the more valuable. They can be ornamented in very many ways. It is a good idea to begin with a covering of paint, plain or patterned paper, or material. Felt is particularly good. Then build up a decoration on top of this from either tiny shells or pebbles, cones, small feathers, beads, buttons or sequins, bits of bark, seeds, pulses, shaped pasta, sand or gravel chips, fashioned into the loveliest design you can create. They can then be given a finishing touch with paint, varnish, or a dusting of glitter. Line the box with felt, and it will make a unique container for a ring, brooch or locket.

Models

Models come in all shapes and sizes. They can be home-made from odds and ends, or bought in antique shops as enormously valuable items. They can range from a rough imitation of an original object, to an absolutely perfect miniature reproduction, accurate in every detail.

So, if you are to become a collector, you will need to decide, right from the beginning, exactly what sort of models are of most interest to you. Generally speaking, model collecting falls into three different categories. You can make the models entirely yourself, you can buy kits and assemble them, or you can collect ready-made models. The choice is entirely yours.

In other sections of this book you can find suggestions about making models of birds, animals and people from fir cones, shells, branches, bottles, stones, and even bus tickets. It's also quite easy to make a collection of models from: paper and thin card; blocks of soap; corks and matchsticks; pipe-cleaners; polystyrene; aluminium foil, crumpled and rolled into shape; packing tubes and egg cartons, as well as from plasticine, traditional modelling clay, and the splendid new synthetic clay which is so much easier to use.

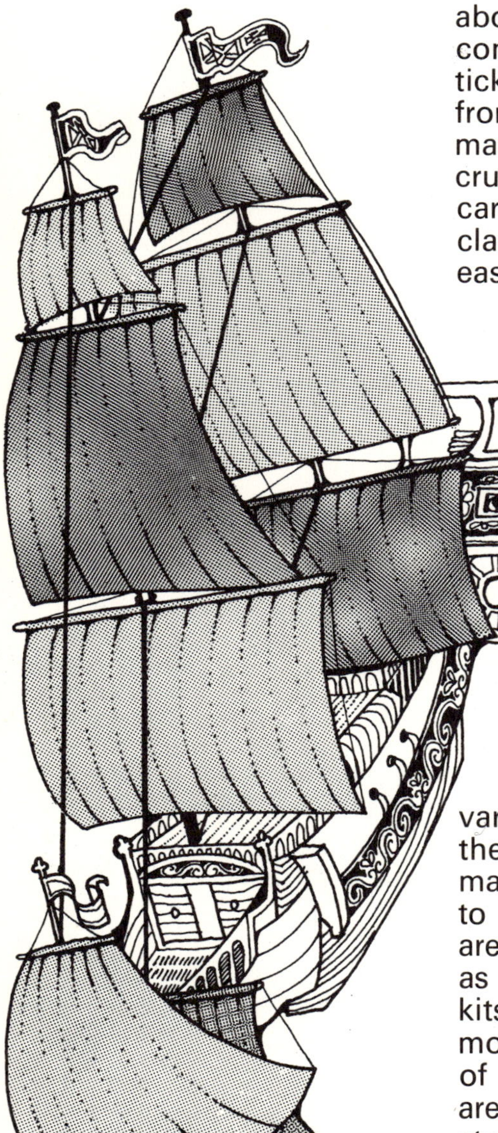

If you would prefer to work from kits you will find a great variety available in model shops and toyshops. Many of them are made in thin card, and this is a particularly good material for models of buildings, ranging from famous ones to simple barns and sheds for a farmyard lay-out. Others are made in balsa wood, which is suitable for model aircraft, as it is light enough to fly well. There are interesting metal kits too, especially in the field of working mechanical models. But nowadays, by far the greatest number are made of plastic, and these cover a huge range of subjects. There are plastic kits of aeroplanes, cars, engines, railway rolling stock, tanks, ships, spacecraft and lunar modules, service men and civilians, dinosaurs, skeletons, wild and domesticated animals, TV characters, and buildings of all sorts.

The two most important things to remember when you are making up a model kit is that you must follow the directions precisely, and you must work neatly. You will need only one or two simple tools, a craft knife, for instance, and a file, the adhesive recommended in the instructions, and some paints for the finishing work. But you will also need a great deal of patience.

If you do not want to take a lot of time and trouble making models, then a collection of ready-made models is the thing for you. Again, there are lots to choose from. You might like to concentrate on miniaturised cars, or dressed dolls, doll's house furniture, historical characters, or military equipment, to name just a few. You could either collect complete series of models, a range of glass or china animals, for instance, or you could choose just one particular subject and see how many different types of model you can find. I know a boy with a passion for penguins. In less than a year he has collected nearly twenty models, ranging from a tiny silver charm to a large stuffed felt penguin, and including examples made from glass, wood, plastic, china and folded paper.

The big problem is knowing how to store and display your collection. If you leave them standing about, or hanging from the ceiling, they tend to collect dust, and it is not an easy job to clean such delicate things. The ideal display unit is a cabinet with glass doors and shelves. You might be able to acquire one that is not in use, or persuade an adult to help you transform an old cupboard by removing some of the wooden panels and replacing them with glass.

If your models are quite small you can keep them in clear orchid boxes, if you can persuade a florist to sell you some, or in the transparent containers that some food is sold in, such as pre-packed tomatoes or large cakes.

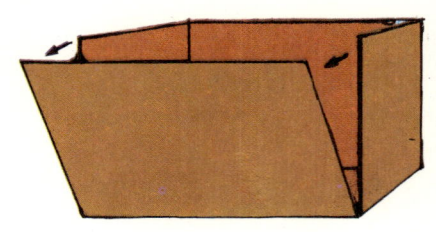

As a setting for your models, make a series of three-dimensional dioramas from large cardboard boxes. With the long side of the box facing you, cut down the front corners from top to bottom, so that the front side folds down flat. Measure a piece of white paper to fit around the other three sides of the interior of the box, and paint a suitable background scene on it, trying to give some impression of distance. Cover the bottom of the box, and the fold-down side, with textured paper, vinyl, felt, or some other material to represent grass, sand, water, concrete, tarmac, or whatever is most appropriate. Add one or two little details to increase the reality of the scene, and place your models in this setting. Place large models at the front and smaller ones towards the back to produce an effective impression of distance and perspective.

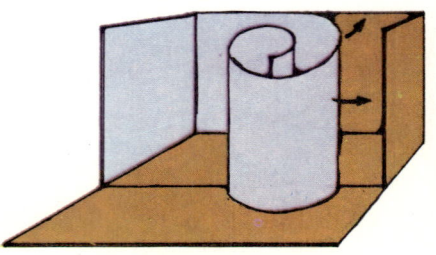

Using this method you could create an airport, a farm-yard, a jungle, a section of motorway, or moon surface, a railway station, or whatever you wish.

If you have an aquarium that is not in use you could make a seascape inside it, rather like the dinosaurium described in the section about bark and twigs. Paint a sea scene on a piece of card and stand it at the back, build up waves out of plaster in the bottom, colouring them green and blue, and set your model ships among them. You might like to add rocks, a lighthouse and a scattering of seagulls to add to the effect.

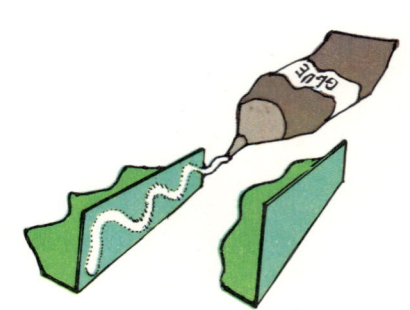

Of course, you can play games with your models if you wish. War-gaming is becoming a very popular hobby. The idea is to use model soldiers and military equipment to recreate famous battles, exactly as they took place, or to work out new examples of military strategy.

If you prefer more peaceful games you could build a lay-out of a town or village in its surrounding countryside, and use model people and animals, buildings and vehicles to create the sort of life that might be lived there today, in the past, or in the future. It could be a place you know well, or one that you have created out of your own imagination.

Model-collecting can be a fascinating hobby, and one that is as old as time. Many museums possess models dating back to the Stone Age, as well as miniature galleys and chariots made by the Ancient Egyptians and Romans. Bone sailing ships, carved by prisoners of the Napoleonic Wars, and Victorian model soldiers and dolls' houses have now become prized collectors' items. I have no doubt at all that some of the beautiful models made today will become the rare and precious antiques of the future.

Stamps & Coins

Stamp and coin collecting, or *philately* and *numismatology*, if you want to give them their proper names, are very popular hobbies throughout the world, for people of all ages. You need quite a lot of specialised knowledge to become an expert in either, and many books have been written about them, both for beginners, and for more experienced collectors.

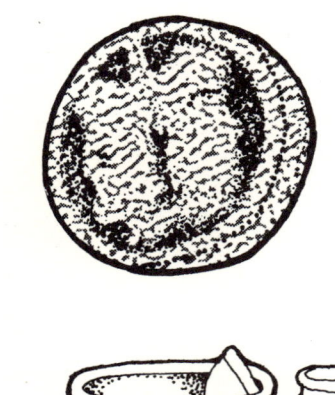

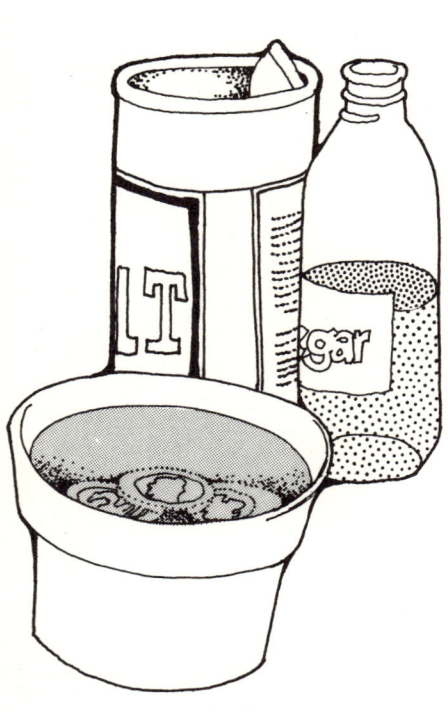

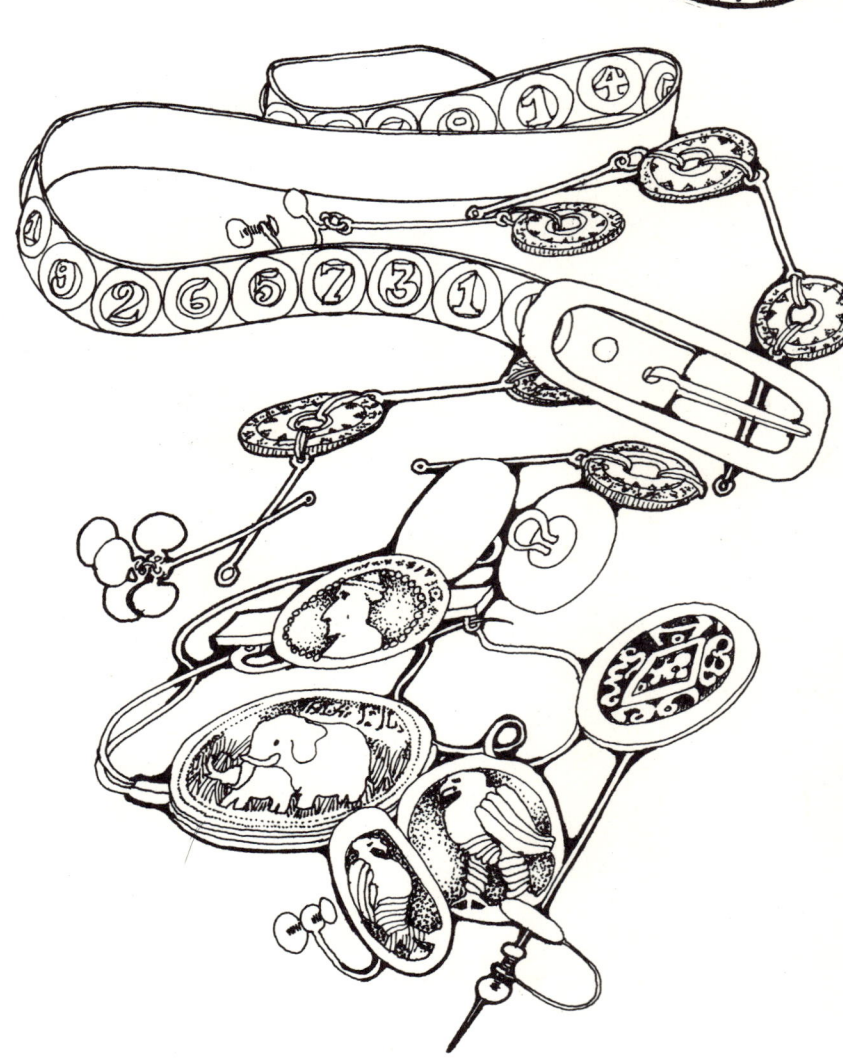

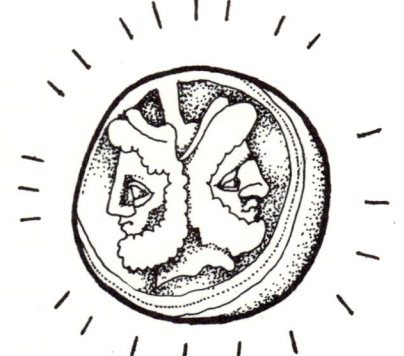

In this book all I have space for are a few ideas for using spare coins and stamps that are not part of a special collection, but have been acquired casually, on holiday, perhaps, or from letters that arrive through the post.

Let us start with coins. On page 37 you can read about using coin rubbings to make a picture, and they could also decorate greetings cards, wrapping paper, or book covers.

Coins are usually well designed and very decorative. If you clean them properly you will find that their colour will improve and they will develop a shine, although cleaning them can reduce their value. Steep them for a short while in a mixture of salt and vinegar, and see for yourself what a difference it makes. Now they will be attractive enough to fasten on to jewellery mounts, from a craft shop, and you will be able to transform them into ear-rings, brooches, bracelets and pendants, tie-pins and cuff-links. Another idea is to stick them on to dressmakers' button bases to make a set of very novel coin buttons.

They can also make a decoration on the sides or lid of a box. For instance, a wooden cigar box, given a coat of paint and then covered in this way, can be transformed into a smart household bills box for your father or mother, a money-box for yourself or a collecting box for a particular charity you support.

If you are interested in how money works, and the way its value is constantly changing throughout the world, you could use a collection of foreign coins to help you to study the money market. Every time you acquire and identify a new coin make a note of the date, and its current value in your own currency. Then, every month, look up the rate of exchange on the financial page of a newspaper and see how its price has altered. You will be astonished at all the differences you have to record in your notebook.

Finally, a few ideas for using up all those postage stamps that come through your letter-box. Remove them from their envelopes by floating them on the surface of a saucer of warm water for a few minutes. After you have peeled them off, dry them out on a piece of newspaper, then press them overnight between the pages of an old book. You can now transform them into unusual pictures.

The easiest way of doing this is to use as your base the outline pictures you find in colouring books, or embroidery transfers reproduced on plain paper. Or you can trace a design, or create one of your own. Fill in the outlines by pasting on complete stamps or bits of stamps of an appropriate colour, building up an interesting textured look by using several different types, and turning them around at angles to each other. A tree, for example, could be filled in with a variety of shades of green, with slivers of brown to indicate branches, and with browns and greys combining for the trunk. When your picture is complete you can mount it on card, varnish the surface, add a ribbon loop for hanging, and perhaps a calendar tab too. Smaller pictures can be transformed into very special greetings cards.

Stamps also make an effective covering for a whole range of household objects. They can turn a plain box, bottle, tin or jar into something very unusual, and you can experiment by creating formal or random patterns, or representative pictures, just as if you were using mosaic. They can ornament a lampshade or wastepaper bin. They can give a new look to an old cracked plate or vase – and hide the crack at the same time. They can cover the sort of papier mâché model described on page 66, and, of course, they can be used to decorate place mats or coasters, a tray, or table-top, window-sill, drawer-front or cupboard door as described in other sections of this book.

Do remember to take the trouble to protect your stamp-craft either with varnish or transparent vinyl before it goes on display. If you have created something beautiful it is sensible to preserve its beauty. And one of the things I hope you will have discovered while you have been reading this book is that there is an enormous amount of beauty to be found in the ordinary objects that surround us in our daily lives. It is yours for the collecting.

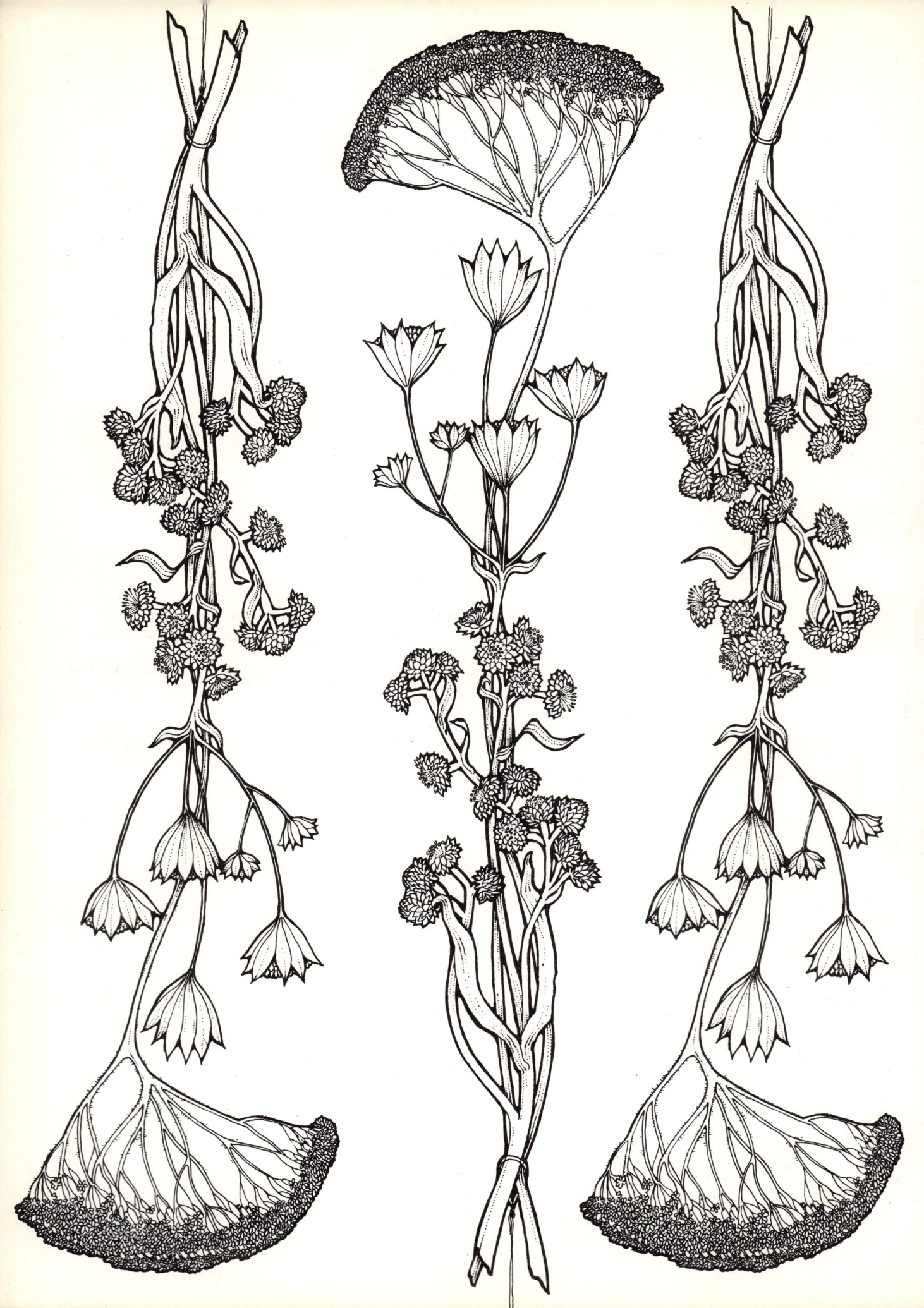